Doorways
to
Holiness

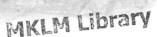

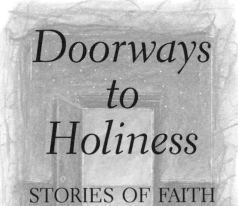

Doorways to Holiness

STORIES OF FAITH

*Jack Rathschmidt, OFM Cap
and Gaynell Cronin*

Paulist Press
New York/Mahwah, N.J.

Cover design by Cynthia Dunne
Cover photograph by Dennis Barloga
Book design by Lynn Else

Library of Congress Cataloging-in-Publication Data

    Rathschmidt, John J.
    Doorways to holiness : Stories of faith / Jack Rathschmidt and Gaynell Cronin.
        p. cm.
    ISBN 0-8091-4373-9 (alk. paper)
    1. Christian life. 2. Faith. I. Cronin, Gaynell Bordes. II. Title.
    BV4501.3.R39 2006
    242—dc22

                                   2005025493

Published by Paulist Press
997 Macarthur Boulevard
Mahwah, New Jersey 07430

www.paulistpress.com

Printed and bound in the
United States of America

Contents

Series Editor's Preface

One of the definitions of *doorway* is "a means of gaining access." In this volume, Gaynell Cronin and Jack Rathschmidt help us gain access in not one but two ways. The stories they tell of real people give us an entrée into the ordinary and yet amazing lives of their acquaintances. Once we are allowed to enter the stories, we are gently challenged to discover how these life experiences can bring us into deeper conversation with a piece of our own life. They reveal and help us discover the hidden richness of our own ordinary experiences, feed our spirituality, and challenge our own lived faith. This is a doorway that swings in both directions: in to discover and learn, out to live and act.

These "Doorways" were written initially as columns for catechists in Paulist Press's *FaithWorks* newsletter. In gathering them together as the first volume in the *FaithWorks* series of books, it was immediately evident that they are not just for catechists. They are clearly for anyone hungry to find connections between the events on the path of life that we walk and our relationships with God and with one another as Christians. You are sure to find treasures behind each doorway.

Jean Marie Hiesberger
April 2005

Introduction

The LORD will keep
your going out and your coming in
from this time on and forevermore. (Ps 121:8)

Most of us know doorway people, friends or family who seem always to be there when we are in transition. Rarely directive or pushy, and never manipulative, they are content to wait for us, no matter how long it takes, to decide, to move, to enter new territory or relationships. Intent without staring, they watch carefully, like lifeguards at a crowded swimming pool, making sure we are safe, warning us about danger but letting us choose our own depth. They are the companions we all need, whose faces appear in every family photo, usually standing quietly at the edges.

My aunt Rita Mae was my doorway person. Once, when visiting my dad during his long last illness, I asked whether he wanted to visit Rita Mae, his youngest sister and always his favorite. Hesitating only a moment, he agreed. When we arrived at Rita Mae's, she was standing in the doorway smiling, arms extended in greeting, despite tending to her own husband who was at home dying. Though clearly anxious, when I suggested that my dad really needed to speak with her, Rita Mae stopped everything, put her face in her hands, asked me to check on her husband Johnny, turned to Dad, and said, "Tell me, Marcel, what's happening?" For the next twenty minutes Aunt Reet never took her eyes from Dad's, and in that short time I discovered again how important unconditional listening is.

That is what doorway people do. They stop. They wait. They listen. Rita Mae's listening not only helped my dad, it changed me. Rita Mae's listening made it possible for me to cross a threshold in acknowledging and naming what was happening in my life, and to begin the process of letting go in order to accept my father's death.

Doorway people, like my aunt Rita Mae, are the foundation of the Christian life. They provide safe passage for coming and going, entering and leaving. Like beautiful crystal or fine china, they bring a special grace to our homes and tables. They are, as this poem suggests,

Doorway Saints

Welcoming strangers
At every doorway,
Calming frightened spirits
With inviting eyes,
Gentling adult children
With a tilt of the head,
Nodding understanding
In every language.
LIKE JESUS

Embracing
Emptiness tenderly,
Witnessing
Faith passionately,
Fighting
Fear peacefully,
Sharing

Good news excitedly.
LIKE JESUS

Massaging hearts
Of tired spirits,
Remembering names
Of forgotten faces,
Patching lives
Torn by neglect,
Praying for all
Despite the cost.
LIKE JESUS

Doorway saints,
You nurture us
By sharing your bread
Touching our wounds
Visiting us in
Prisons of our own making
And loving us
Unconditionally.
LIKE JESUS

Doorways through which we pass over and over again are vulnerable, sometimes fragile places that sometimes fill us with anxiety and fear. Because we so often resist change and avoid moving from the known to the unknown, from the familiar to the unfamiliar, they can appear like thick, high walls. Whether they invite us to come in, stay out, or be wary or excited, they are thresholds that mark our front and back doors, living rooms, bedrooms, kitchens, patios, porches, decks, schools, churches, stores and airplanes, hospitals, restaurants, retreats and counseling centers.

The people who stand in our doorways, waiting to see our face, to touch us gently and to feed our spirit, are vital to our personal and communal health. In our view, catechists, the people with whom we most often work and always admire, are the first people we think of when we imagine what it means to be doorway people. Welcoming seekers, especially children, unconditionally and giving them an assurance of safety and security, they make it possible not only to relax but to dream, pray, and learn. Catechists, simply by waiting quietly in the doorways of their classrooms and homes, remind us that even though we may feel very distant from God, we have only to realize that it was us who twisted away from God's loving embrace. Like Jesus, they are the "gate," the doorway, through whom we reenter the holy.

But it is not only catechists who function as doorkeepers. Grandparents and parents, aunts and uncles, friends, even enemies, can be doorway people, reminding us every day that God, the ever-faithful Doorkeeper, is always active among us. Like Mary, the sister of Lazarus, God waits at our doorways and sits at our feet. When we are anxious about our fears, dreams, and joys, God holds us close, a Shepherd promising to find us when we are lost and to bring us home to a safe place, laying down his life, if necessary, to protect us through the long night. Like Moses leading his people from slavery to freedom, banging on rocks so that we might drink and climbing mountains to proclaim good news to all who come in need, God is our advocate and our breath, the one who promises us life forever. Our only task, these essays suggest, is to be God's face, hands, heart, and voice. That is all, and that is enough.

The Scriptures remind us of this by speaking more than two hundred times of gates and doorways. Jesus tells us directly "to come in through the narrow gate," to trust him as the gate itself, and to remember that only robbers climb over gates in order to steal other people's sheep.

Imagine gates and doorways mentioned throughout Scripture. Was there a small gate or doorway leading to the animal's pen in which Jesus was born? Did it give Mary and Joseph a sense of security? What did the doors and gates look like that led into the room where Jesus changed water into wine at Cana? Were they guarding the home of poor people, hanging tenuously like the lives of the people themselves? What about the door to the upper room in which Jesus celebrated his last supper? Was it beautifully decorated, inviting all who entered to celebrate the Passover with joy and hope?

Using doorways both as actual thresholds and as metaphors for a new understanding of everyday life, this book explores the holiness of those faithful heroines and heroes who welcome us and especially our children to the exploration of how God is present within and among us on a daily basis. You may even find your own story as a doorway person here. What we suggest is simple: those who are privileged to offer a ministry of hospitality to others will do it well and grow in authentic holiness if they learn first to pay attention to the doorways through which they have walked, especially in their own homes.

Divided into four sections, this book helps us remember those who *welcomed* us with *gratitude*, and accompanied us with *compassion* through every *loss* and joy. It also provides us with a lens through which to understand our relationship to the holy more deeply. Through the doorways of our own homes, lives, and hearts we are sent as apostles to be, both personally and communally, lights in the world. Doorways and doorway people are a marvelous invitation to transformation and growth in the spiritual life.

Finally, please use this book in any way you like.

- Read it alone or with others.

- Skip from section to section.

- Read a reflection a day, or several, until one strikes you as sent from God.

We hope you take your time and do not rush.

- Read slowly, even twice.

- Pray slowly, too, even three times.

When you have more time,

- Use the reflective questions for discussion or to journal and enter more deeply into the mystery of God's presence in your life.

We trust you will find your friends, your family, your enemies, and yourself in these pages. When you do, rejoice. God is whispering ever so gently: "You are precious in my eyes…and I love you" (Isa 43:4).

Doorways of
Welcome

Welcoming strangers at every doorway,…
Nodding understanding at every language.
(Like Jesus)

Welcoming others, indeed, welcoming all of life, is a believer's sacred duty, trust, and mission. To stand in awe and wonder in every doorway waiting to welcome all people as guests sent by God is the first moment of the spiritual journey. We are made in the image of the One who welcomes us, despite our faults and sins, like the forgiving father (Luke 15:11–32) who can't wait to throw a coat around our shoulders and put a ring on our finger, or the new bride (Rev 19:7) dressed in fine linen, so anxious to make a home for her new husband.

The reflections that follow, *Doorways of Welcome*, are about ordinary people who live the gospel a day at a time. As they welcome and provide a safe physical, emotional, and spiritual listening place for all those who visit them, they embody the welcoming face of God we meet throughout the Scriptures. Like the Jesus of Luke's Gospel (9:11), even when they want to escape for a well-deserved rest, they welcome those who seek them for healing and hope. In gratitude for what is, and not in anger because of what has not happened in their lives, they, like all the people in this book, are the everyday saints whose stories need to be told. Symbols of joy, their stories help us read and pray about our own lives, and they remind us of the need not only to offer hospitality and a welcoming presence for others, but also to be kind and gentle with ourselves.

Grandma's Place

See, the home of God
is among mortals. (Rev 21:3)

Grandma's was a special place when I was a young girl. Her home was full of sights, sounds, smells, and energy, and we visited there every Sunday to talk, listen, eat, and remember who we were. Though often the same from week to week, what today's young people might call "boring," I loved going to Grandma's. Her home, and especially the sight of her noodles hanging on the clothesline to dry, filled me with security and a deep sense of belonging. I knew, though I would often feel lonely in life, I would never be alone. Grandma, Uncle Albert, Aunt Reet, Uncle Johnny, Dad, Mom, and all my cousins, despite our roller coaster lives, would always live inside me.

One of Grandma's special qualities was her willingness to welcome visitors as if they were family. She often told us to bring anyone we liked to Sunday dinner. One Sunday I brought my very best friend Miriam, but when Grandma, whose voice and arms seemed big enough to encircle the world, paid more attention to my friend than me, I decided not to invite her again.

I often think about that day and the night that followed. Both were so full of confusing feelings of envy and fear that I had a difficult time sleeping. When I saw Miriam at school, I did not want to speak with her. Though she tried to catch my eye and whisper thanks, I just turned away, grateful for once that the rules prohibited talking after the first bell. What was happening to me? Why was I so uncomfortable? How would I tell my friend that I did not want her to come to Grandma's again?

Jealousy and envy, common feelings in all of us, wounded me. Though I never acted on them and continued to welcome my friend whenever she asked to visit Grandma's, I knew something was different within me and that these hostile forms of self-pity needed healing. For the first time, I understood James and John arguing about who would sit at Jesus' right hand (Mark 10:35–40). More important I also felt growing in me what I would later identify as a new determination to live the good news by welcoming, even seeking out, those most in need of family.

Sometimes, like James and John, children who come to us for faith formation want to be the "apple of our eye." In their need to be noticed and the center of attention, they are often jealous of the recognition we give others. Like me with Grandma, they want an exclusive friendship.

How often we have had this experience with a friend or spouse, only to realize that our love, like God's love and Grandma's love, must be expansive. Only then can we invite all to come and gather under the protective shade of the mustard tree whose branches offer shelter and safety, an inclusive dwelling place for all.

My sin, my fault, was, as Augustine says, a "happy" one. It taught me about my own ability to exclude, hurt, and withdraw from others. Though I might want to think it was because Miriam was receiving more attention than me, in fact I had received a badly needed sign about my own smallness that I would treasure for a lifetime. I understood and was grateful for the sentiment of Dostoevsky: "one memory from childhood is your best education." I still live from that memory.

Prayer

Grandma God,
Some of yesterday's feelings have become today's "I feel petty"—
that confused place between envy and fear. Is this possessive self
me? May your arms and voice encircle me…and everyone. Make
me…us, the "apple of your eye." In your expansive and inclusive
friendship, God of All, be with me…us, as we welcome and seek
those in need of Grandma's place. Amen.

Doorway Reflections

- Who are the grandmas in your life?
- What safe belonging place do you call home?
- How do you acknowledge your possessive self?
- How do you attend to and heal your wounds of jealous envy, exclusivity?
- What can we do, should we do, when envious and jealous feelings seem to possess us rather than us possessing them?
- Ask someone about how she or he handles difficult feelings.

 # Doorkeeper

Then the watcher called out:
"Upon the watchtower, I stand, O LORD,
continually by day, and at my post I am
stationed throughout the night." (Isa 21:8)

Exceedingly thin and wiry, Tommy was only seven when I first met him. Hardly what one would expect from a PINS (Person in Need of Support) child, he had been sent to the Children's

Village, a home for emotionally disturbed boys, by the courts. He smiled easily but almost never looked directly at me or any other adult except to check out my reaction to his behavior. When he came each week to our chapel for religious education, he sat to the side of the room, never directly in my line of sight, and rarely said a word.

Neither did Tommy seem to learn very much. If I asked him a specific question, he would smile but say nothing. When I asked him if he understood me, he raised his eyebrows slightly but kept silent. The other boys neither spoke to him nor paid him any attention.

One Sunday, when many families were visiting, I noticed Tommy hanging around the chapel. As parents stopped to ask about their sons, Tommy listened from a distance. Throughout the afternoon he was never far from the front door of the chapel. After a while, he opened the door for visitors, pretending he was on duty in order to keep listening to the questions and comments of the adults present.

The following week I learned that Tommy had lived in six foster homes. Coming to the chapel on Sundays or anyplace else where adults gathered helped him. Tommy became our "keeper of the door" for the next ten months. Every Sunday he would get to the chapel early to hold the door open for the congregation. After a while, he began to say, "Good morning. Have a nice day." When people answered him, Tommy glowed. He was becoming socialized, learning in the simplest possible way how to greet others.

Jewish tradition appointed someone to be keeper of the threshold, to stand in the in-between, a vulnerable, fearful point where one waits and is challenged to step into the unknown. Tommy became our keeper of the threshold, much like the

Peruvian Dominican St. Martin de Porres. In his duties as a porter, St. Martin gave food and clothing to the poor each day. He was the doorkeeper, welcoming the unwanted, the unloved, and the destitute. Standing at his door, his in-between place, he found the face of Jesus in the poor, and helped people believe in themselves again.

For Tommy the church slowly became his home, his community, his family; and the church door became his sentry post. Tommy belonged, had a role, and found a path at the church door. When he finally celebrated first Eucharist several months later, five different adults asked if they could hold the door open for Tommy that day. Not only had Tommy found a ministry at the chapel door, he had mentored others as well.

Prayer

Doorkeeper God,
When you visit, let me open the door of my heart, give you a hint of a smile, and then listen to discover what you want me to know and accept about myself. I yearn to belong and do not know how. The in-between frightens me. Gently hold the Tommy that is within me and the Tommys I meet every day. Together may we greet and be greeted by one another. Amen.

Doorway Reflections

- Who are the Tommys in your life? How do you open and close doors? Who stands with you in the *in-between*?
- Isaiah reminds us that the sentry stands guard day and night. What are the qualities of a doorkeeper? What door is a sentry post in your ministry? How are you the keeper of the door to your heart and to God's presence there? Who taught you to

greet and welcome others? How do you need others to greet you right now?

Doorways of Sound

You know what time it is, how it is now the moment for you to wake from sleep.
(Rom 13:11)

When I was a young boy, the sisters who administered our school rang a bell several times a day signaling us to pause for a few moments in prayer. It was a time for quiet and reflection, a reminder that we were not alone. Although it now seems somewhat artificial and manipulative, in many ways it helped us students to absorb a fundamental truth about our faith tradition: God is ever-alert to us, anxious to hear our concerns, needs, and dreams. We have only to pause for a few moments to remember God as an unconditionally loving parent who cannot forget us.

In recent years, I have used my watch in much the same way. Since I am a gadget person, my watch not only tells time; it has six alarms, a timer, and a memory that stores thirty phone numbers. Though it is very unattractive, I love my watch with all its functions.

A couple of years ago, when a good friend was diagnosed with cancer, I promised to pray with him each day when he went for chemotherapy. To keep my pledge, I set one of my watch alarms for 2:00 p.m., the exact time Charlie's cancer treatments began. One day I was with a group of peer ministers in the campus ministry office at the college where I work when the alarm sounded. I stopped speaking immediately, paused, and then looked again at the students. "Are you okay, Brother Jack?" Alma asked. "Yes, I'm fine. I promised a friend with cancer to pray for him each day at 2:00 p.m. That's when his treatments begin." The students were respectful and intrigued.

Several days later, when my alarm went off again, Alma stopped speaking, bowed her head in silence for a few moments, then smiled at me. "We'll pray together," she said. I was moved and grateful.

More important, in a few weeks, this simple custom spread throughout our campus ministry team. Each time my watch alarm sounded, we would pause. Additionally, if a guest was present, someone would tell her or him that we were praying for the sick. It all felt very natural. Just last week, visiting with a former colleague, my alarm sounded and she asked, "Who are we praying for today?" Similarly, the Buddhist monk Thich Nhat Hanh introduced the ringing of a bell in his community, alerting people to pause and take three mindful breaths.

Customs like this are very helpful and necessary for our children. Hungry for ways to incorporate spiritual practices in their lives, they take easily and quickly to habits that remind them to be aware of God and one another. Moreover, these customs take us out of our tendency toward self-absorption. Remembering others who are sick or in need grounds us in our faith community and challenges us to let go of the anxieties and cares that sometimes strangle us with worry.

Jesus constantly reminded his followers to be alert to God's presence. The women waiting for the bridegroom's return (Matt 25:13) and the disciples in the garden of Gethsemane (Matt 26:41) are urged to "stay awake" and pray. C. S. Lewis echoes the same message: "The world is crowded with God. The real labor is to remember, to attend. In fact, to come awake. Still more. To remain awake." Indeed, as Paul's letter to the Romans suggests, it is the time, the hour, to awake from our sleep and notice (Rom 13:11).

Prayer

Gracious One,
You crowd our world. Wherever we turn, we find your face. Awaken us from our sleep. Alert us to your presence and make us aware of the needs of your people. In the sounding of a watch or bell, sweep away our self-absorption and open our hearts to what is happening here, now, in this moment. Pause with us as we take three mindful breaths of your life within and among us. Amen.

Doorway Reflections

- What signals you to pause and turn to God in your daily living? Like the alarm on the watch, do you have a custom that has spread throughout your family or group?
- How do you pray for people who are ill?
- How and when would you engage in the practice of three mindful breaths during your day?
- In what ways is your world "crowded with God"?

 # An Old Green Door

O taste and see that the LORD *is good.*
(Ps 34:8)

The last leg of the trip to Interlaken, New York, where we vacation every year with family and friends, snakes along Lake

Cayuga, finally opening up and revealing a beautiful, long, wide body of water and *Shadow Lawn*, the boat house that sits on a spit of land that extends into the lake itself.

As soon as I see the boat house the questions come. Should we unload food supplies first? Drive to the back of the property, make beds, and get settled? Stop and sit for a few moments in gratitude that the almost five-hour trip was safe?

My choice is always the same. Pushing open the old green door, I walk through the boat house and slide open the door to the dock, letting in the light and air that so refresh me. Then I step onto the dock, walk around noting any changes since last we were there, and pray in gratitude for the opportunity to do nothing for an entire week.

As children and adults rush about putting food in pantries and refrigerators, I breathe in more than thirty years of memories. I vacationed at Interlaken as a college student with other young friars, glad to be free of the study and work that so consumed us as young men and returned often for retreats with candidates to our community. Now I have the exquisite pleasure of living simply with the people I love most for a week of relaxation and refreshment. Walking through the doors of *Shadow Lawn* opens and reopens possibility, hope, and renewal for me and all who gather there. How beautiful that old green door appears to me!

Although the Scriptures tell us that Jesus regularly escaped to mountaintops and "the other side of the lake" (Matt 8:18) for prayer and rest, they say little about what we call vacation. Perhaps the lives of people in New Testament times had more of a rhythm to them than ours, but the wedding feast at Cana, where Jesus celebrated with friends and family, suggests much about what vacations could be.

In the Jewish culture of Jesus' day, marriages were special times. Though often very poor, entire villages stopped working, crowned the soon-to-be married couple with flowers, led them from home to home, and hailed them as king and queen for as long as the celebration lasted. Mary's plea that Jesus help the young couple whose party would be over when the wine ran out helps us remember not only her compassion but her challenge to care for those most in need. Stopping in our everyday lives to rest a while, enjoy our families and friends, and remember how much God loves a party and us is holy.

All work and no play is a recipe for disaster. Unless we take time to enjoy how God is working within and among us, our ability to welcome others with joy and hope, so central to all ministry, will be sorely tested.

Prayer

Companion God,
We remember and give thanks for the happenings of summer and for the green doors of our lives. Bless us as your doorway people. Help us paint doors of green to welcome your people as they come to the places where we learn, pray, and grow in faith. Together, let us taste and see your goodness as we rest together. Amen.

Doorway Reflections

- Do you take time to relax and refresh yourself, to "see and taste the goodness of God"? What makes you stop and sit for a few moments in gratitude?
- Reflect on your own green door of vacations and how these renewed your ministry. Where is your Shadow Lawn, your safe

resting place for breathing in memories and hope? Take a few moments to enjoy how God is working within you right now.

Doorway of No Excuse

Give light to my eyes…
I trusted in your steadfast love. (Ps 13:3, 5)

Bernice was ninety-two and feisty. A woman of great integrity and intelligence, she had loved a party as a younger woman, but in recent years felt intimidated having to get ready for big events. After looking through her wardrobe, doubting she could find anything appropriate, she would decline most invitations. Though bright and witty, Bernice wondered if she really fit any longer. Obsessing about what to wear was a very convenient excuse.

When her friends Peter and Mary invited her to their fortieth wedding anniversary, Bernice initially accepted but a week before the celebration she called saying she didn't feel well. Not wanting to embarrass her, Peter and Mary accepted her excuse but told her they would call in a few days to see if she had changed her mind. Her presence, they assured her, would make their party complete. Finally, Bernice relented, went to the party, and had a marvelous time, welcoming excited children to her table, clapping for the young people as they danced, and sharing her wonderful stories.

As my mother grew older, she told me similar stories. While she wanted to be involved in her children's lives, she was not sure that she really fit. Her hearing had always been poor and her osteoporosis made her back very round. While she had a brace to help her at home, she hated to wear it in public. It attracted too much attention. Besides none of her clothes fit properly over the brace. Like Bernice, my mother's clothes became the excuse she often used to absent herself from public life.

Children often provide the elderly with a gentle path through these kinds of struggles. My niece Lynn had only to ask my mother once for Mom to agree enthusiastically to any request. Mom knew that Lynn saw her beauty and goodness, delighted in talking with her, and bragged often to her friends that her grandma was her best friend. Though Mom knew Lynn was exaggerating, she did not doubt that Lynn genuinely enjoyed being with her no matter how she looked or how often she had to ask her to repeat something she had not heard.

Both Bernice and my mom need their friends and children to honor their wisdom and search for ways to include them in celebrations. We all need to look beyond our excuses and rely on our intuitive sense of what is right. Jesus was very good at this important skill. When the Samaritan woman at the well tried to hide her sin from him, Jesus challenged her in a way that sent her back to her townsfolk proclaiming Jesus' prophetic ability and asking: "Could this be the Christ?" (John 4:29). We can all be Christ for the elderly and for those who feel that they don't fit any longer by looking beyond their fears and reluctance to the wisdom they possess in so much abundance.

Prayer

God of No Excuses,
Clothe me in courage. Crowds alarm me. Sometimes I feel like a
burden and do not fit anywhere like I once did. What's appropri-
ate now in what one wears, in how one feels, in what one says? My
great temptation is to get out of the way and let others live their

lives. But then I think of the Peters, Marys, and Lynns who see our beauty and goodness and I pray with the psalmist, thanking you for giving me through others a sparkle in my eyes again. God of all clothes, rid and deliver me from convenient excuses. Let me wear and trust in your steadfast love and help me to be among the young regardless of how I look and sound. Let me discover, honor, and share the wisdom that is mine. Amen.

Doorway Reflections

- How do you handle getting ready, finding appropriate clothes for big events?
- Reflect on a time when you looked beyond someone's excuses, and like Mary and Peter persisted in including that person.
- Consider the excuses you make when fearful. What are the symbols of your own discomfort in a new situation?
- Like Lynn and Jesus with the Samaritan woman, whose beauty and goodness do you notice? Who notices yours? How do you look at the elderly? Who brings sparkle to your eyes again?

Retreat Center Doors

You are near, O LORD.
(Ps 119:151)

As a young woman, Rita made weekend retreats regularly and loved them. Feeling very close to God, especially through nature, she also enjoyed the quiet and stillness of the retreat center grounds. Though not always sure she understood everything the retreat director said, she listened closely and usually found something to benefit her life. Making a retreat was like closing her bedroom door at night. She felt safe, secure, and relaxed.

Now almost fifty, Rita was finally treating herself to another weekend away. She was more anxious than she expected, and the drive to the retreat center seemed long. Though a practicing Catholic, she had changed a great deal over the years. She wondered why the Church was so slow to ordain women and married men, and often found herself speechless in the face of violence in the world. Was a retreat center really the place for her to go?

When she finally saw the signs for the retreat center, she relaxed a little. Walking through the front door, she met the familiar smell of incense and in a few moments she was directed to her room. Washing her face, she had the distinct feeling that the fears she had in the car were draining away and she was very grateful.

As she sat down at the small desk in her room, she was flooded with peace. Though she had made her share of mistakes, hers was a good life. Her children were healthy and faith filled. One even volunteered at a local nursing home. Though her husband worked too many hours and they sometimes took each other for granted, her problems were small.

Leafing through the Bible, a passage from St. Luke's Gospel caught her eye: "Consider the ravens: they neither sow nor reap; they have no storeroom or barn, yet God feeds them. Of how much more value are you than birds! And can any of you by worrying add a single hour to your span of life?" (12:24). God is wonderfully, powerfully near when God feeds us. Is not prayer, then, like a meal, an intimate sharing between friends, a time to be alone with God who loves and wants to be with us? Rita knew she had made a good decision and with a very light heart went downstairs to the first retreat conference.

All of us know we need to take time to rest, reflect, and honor God through quiet prayer but finding or making the time can be very difficult. St. Francis de Sales once wrote: "A half hour of meditation a day is essential except when you are very busy. Then a full hour is demanded." When was the last time you spent quiet time with God? Have you ever made a weekend retreat? The number of us who answer negatively to both questions is startling. Today might be a good day to reconsider our priorities.

Prayer

Friend Jesus,
I know you are near. Move me to quiet and stillness, to an inti-
mate closeness with you. Like a mother bathing her child, wash
away my acute fears and anxieties. Intimate One, make me light
hearted and fill me with gratitude for the time to rest and be
alone with you. Give me moments to reflect and let my prayer be
a door that opens into the mystery of you as friend and compan-
ion, into an always nearness and thereness. Flood me with your
life. Amen.

Doorway Reflections

- When do you feel close to God?
- How do you pay attention to the nearness of God daily?
- When and where are you able to have quiet and stillness?
- Like Rita, what motivates and urges you to take time away?
- Consider planning a retreat time for yourself at home or away. In what ways could or does this time benefit you and your

relationship with God? Is your retreat experience today different from or similar to earlier retreats? What do you need to wash away?

Bedroom Doors

In the morning my prayer comes before you.
(Ps 88:13)

Carol was startled by her alarm clock. Usually a light sleeper, she couldn't believe it was 6:45 a.m. Time to rise, shower, dress, and serve a quick breakfast to Jared and Emily before dropping them off at day care and fighting traffic into the city to be at work by 8:30 a.m.

Carol hated days like this. A single mother, she worked very hard to steal a few minutes each morning before the children woke to sit quietly in her bedroom and ask God for help with her life and day. Today she would have to rush. Frustrated by oversleeping, she also felt the old resentment toward her husband, who had announced eight months earlier that he was leaving. His job, two small children, and his inability to communicate with Carol were too much for him. Refusing Carol's offer to seek counseling, he simply packed his clothes and left.

Stifling tears of self-pity, Carol jumped from bed and bolted for the shower, only to be stopped by the small Celtic cross on the back of her bedroom door. Inscribed with the words "Peace be with you. My peace I leave with you," it also had an old slip of paper tacked to the door below the cross. On it were words written in her own hand, "And God protect the children, my own and those who come to me for religious education."

Carol stopped and breathed deeply for almost a minute. Her spirit would no longer allow her to rush through the doorway. Knowing she would not return to her bedroom for sixteen hours, she thanked God for the deep sleep she experienced, asked for the courage to forgive her husband, and smiled as she listened to the playful noises of her children in the next room. "Okay, God," she whispered, "you win again. Walk with me and us today. Help me pay attention to you in all people I meet and places I enter. Forgive my complaining and free me from self-absorption."

Carol's day, which had begun in chaos, had changed in less than a minute. Pausing in her bedroom doorway, she was refreshed by the One who is always with us. Bedrooms are special places. Paying attention to them, especially through our bodies and senses, can be a fruitful spiritual exercise.

While Scripture speaks of the trumpet call in the morning awakening and welcoming people into the day of the Lord, our culture is often marked by alarm clocks, radios, and wake-up calls. Can you hear Isaiah's challenge, "Morning by morning he wakens—wakens my ear" (50:4)? Thich Nhat Hanh echoes Isaiah's call: "Waking up this morning, I smile. Twenty four brand new hours before me. I vow to live fully in each moment. And to look at all beings with eyes of compassion." Because we know that each morning is different, we ask ourselves: What will we be taught today? What will we see and hear of God? Each day, if we are open, we can hear God's voice anew.

Prayer

Morning God,
Give me the grace to greet the newness of a day with a smile, and to listen to your word. Awaken my mind and heart to live fully each

*moment. Set my direction to walk over the threshold of my bed-
room door into your world and to look at and serve all people with
eyes of compassion. And when I return to my bedroom tonight,
make it a place of safety and rest. Amen.*

Doorway Reflections

- How do you begin your day in your bedroom?
- What gesture helps you focus, set the tone, and appreciate the
  beginning of a day?
- Where and what are your doorway reminders of God's presence?
- What words would you inscribe on your door that speak of
  your ministry and those to whom you minister?

Doors of Waiting

*While he was still far off, his father saw him
and was filled with compassion.* (Luke 15:20)

Jose blushed deeply as Anselma, the director of religious education, praised him effusively during a prayer service. Reminding
everyone that no one had been able to control, much less teach,
the seventh- and eighth-grade class for the past several years,
Anselma looked directly at Jose as she told us how wonderful and
welcoming he was. Not only was he a man of faith, she insisted,
he was a gentle yet demanding teacher who led his students in
generous acts of service among the poorest people of their little
town. Unable to look up, Jose accepted Anselma's praise but it
was clear that he had not sought her recognition and would have
felt much better without it.

What Anselma didn't mention was that Jose was a seventy-eight-year-old widower whose wife of fifty-five years had died only four months previously. Jose was grieving deeply. When I spoke with Jose after the service, he told me his moving and humbling story. He and Carla had moved to their small home in southeast Texas five years ago to escape the speed of Houston. Both of them had been active in the church for decades as catechists, lectors, and extraordinary ministers of the Eucharist.

But it had not always been so. Jose assured me that his wife Carla was the heart of his family. While they had been married for fifty-five years, he had only really been present for thirty-five of them. Jose was a recovering alcoholic who, for almost twenty years, rarely went home, much less to church. His wife had endured his absences with great dignity. If anyone deserved to be praised, he assured me, it was she. Because Carla and God had never given up on him, he could never give up on young people, especially those struggling with the trials of adolescence.

While most of us do not suffer directly from the terrible disease of alcoholism, we all bear some heavy burden. In fact, the biggest minority in our country are those with disabilities, people who must manage burdens as diverse as dyslexia and paralysis. What Jose teaches us is that despite our struggles, God is never far from us and is always waiting for our return like the forgiving father of Luke's Gospel (Luke 15).

The ability to wait patiently is a precious gift. Nelson Mandela endured decades in jail as he waited for his own freedom and the liberation of the people of South Africa. The Dalai Lama continues to wait for the opportunity to return to Tibet. No amount of arguing could convince these men that they should give up, forget their dreams, and find a different path to God. Despite suffering terribly, their commitment to the truth, their belief in the goodness of the human spirit, and their confidence in God are the only strengths they need to remain faithful to their convictions.

No doubt our compulsion to teach, parent, or live well sometimes gets in the way of our listening to others' lives. Nevertheless, the biblical stories of God's faithfulness and the witness of the saints assure us that nothing is more important than listening in nurturing faith-filled children.

Prayer

God of All Waitings,
The words of Nelson Mandela echo deep inside: "The time for heal-
ing of the wounds has come. The time to build is upon us. There is
no easy road to freedom. We must therefore act together as a united
people for reconciliation." Like Mandela, let us not forget the dreams
you, O God, have planted deep inside. Commit us to truth. Awaken
our belief in the goodness of the human spirit. Convict us to faith-
fulness. You are never far from us, God. Like the forgiving Father you
wait ever so patiently for our return home—with all our weaknesses
and frailties. Embrace us and give us the gift of patient waiting. Like
Carla, never give up on us. Amen.

Doorway Reflections

- Who are the people struggling in your own life?
- Is there a heavy burden that you carry?
- Who has never given up on you?
- How are you present to the grieving?
- Do you take time to praise others for the work they do?
- Consider the ways you might help the grieving to do generous acts of service.

- Pray a gospel story of God's faithfulness with others, tell your own, and listen to the stories of others.

A Gate of Welcome

Come in now to your home, and welcome, with blessing and joy. (Tob 11:17)

Though no longer young, I had always prided myself for being in good shape. But major surgery and too much work began to catch up with me. I had gained a few pounds, sometimes felt winded going up stairs, and too often needed to go to bed earlier than I liked. Since I had never been a runner or played sports formally, I decided to go to the local fitness club to reclaim my health and, I hoped, my independence.

What a revelation! Almost everyone at the club was young, at least younger than I. Nevertheless, despite the incessant music and other distractions all around me, I was determined to begin. The program I joined offered two free sessions with an experienced trainer, in my case a former dancer who looked wonderful in leotard and tights. Determined not to be intimidated, I listened to her for a few minutes and then began to feel small and foolish. Her tone was patronizing and judgmental as she told me that I should not try certain machines until I was in better shape. It was not so much what she said that disturbed and upset me, it was the way she said it. I listened as closely as I could but, feeling very vulnerable, excused myself.

Driving home that evening, I suddenly realized how many young parents, trying their best to raise their children in faith, must feel in church, particularly when returning after a long absence. The language, the space, the ritual, and the music are all foreign to them. Did they, like me at the fitness club, simply listen politely, too confused to ask questions, and escape to the safety of their home and neighborhoods, hoping to get through whatever programs we demanded they attend? I hoped not, but had to admit that my own experience had traumatized me. Why should it be different for them in church?

Jesus warned us about situations like this. Disturbed and angered with the demands of the Pharisees, he almost shouts: "They tie up heavy burdens and lay them on people's shoulders but they will not lift a finger to help them" (Matt 23:4).

Conversely, the book of Tobit reminds us how we are to welcome others. Sent on a journey by his blind father Tobit, Tobias returns to Nineveh not only with medicine to shrink his father's cataracts, but with Sarah his new bride. Rejoicing that God has restored his sight and eager to share his joy, Tobit runs to the village gate to welcome Sarah and offer her a blessing: "Welcome to your new home. May you always be blessed with good health and happiness."

Like so many, I am in search of that gate and people like Tobit who offer me a blessing and a place to restore my health and happiness. In our ministry we know how important it is to regularly to check our tone of voice, our attitudes, and our easy judgments. Too often I have heard all young people dismissed as "yuppies" or materialists who gladly place their children in day care while they pursue their own careers and agendas. My experience at the health club, viewed through the words of Jesus and Tobit, reminds me how vulnerable we all can be when we start something new. How important it is to welcome all those who come to us for faith formation with gentleness and reverence.

Prayer

God of Health and Happiness,
Afraid. Vulnerable. Confused. Intimidated. Winded. Tired.
Weary. I feel small and foolish. Tears come and I run away. I am
spent: physically, emotionally, spiritually. Restore my health with
your hands of compassion and care. Make me faithful to a fitness
plan of gentleness and reverence in the slow process of healing—
for myself and all the earth. Amen.

Doorway Reflections

- What or who intimidates us in our fitness plan for prayer and action?
- Do we provide a welcoming door and space to help others overcome their fear and vulnerability to the new and unfamiliar? What is our tone of voice and attitude toward the people we serve?
- Do we "tie up heavy burdens...and lay them on the shoulders of others," so that they will need more than a fitness club to restore them to health again?

 # A Place of Presence

For where your treasure is, there your heart
will be also. (Matt 6:19)

Thirty years old and married with three children, Vera had helped around the church for a decade. She loved the musty smell of burning candles and felt very close to God every time she entered what she called her "second home." While her friends sometimes wondered about her priorities, Vera knew what she needed and wanted. Not unlike nuns in their cloisters, the quiet and routine of cleaning centered her and prepared her to be more present to her children and husband.

Vera was grateful to be a wife and mother. Although her family might be able to afford a few more luxuries if she had a job outside her home, neither she nor her husband wanted that. Don wanted his children to have their mother around all the time, especially when they were young. Because Don's parents had been divorced when he was four, his mother was forced to work long hours. Don often came home from school to an empty house and didn't like it. Don's stories hurt Vera, especially when she remembered her mother's welcoming after-school hug, and she wanted to give her children the same love and nurturing she had received.

While few families in contemporary society seem able to afford this kind of lifestyle, Vera and Don offer us interesting and intriguing possibilities and questions. How do we get ourselves centered for the primary work of our lives, whether we stay home or go out to work? If we could design a lifestyle completely to our liking, what would it look like?

The Scriptures offer clear challenges in this regard. "For where your treasure is, there your heart will be also," Jesus says. The *Catechism of the Catholic Church* reminds us that affection and connection among family members is the result of their respect for each other (#2206). In other words, families must spend time with one another, listening compassionately to one another's stories. Without this time spent together, the family's basic religious purpose—to be church, a sign of God's presence in the world—will be lost. Our lifestyle tells much about who we are becoming as people, family, church, and world. At the very least, we need to listen to people like Vera, whose lives speak loudly about a fundamental aspect of gospel living: community. Our families are called to be the first communities of faith, reflection, and service we enter. From family we move into the larger church and world. That we sometimes delude ourselves into believing we can do this without spending time together in our homes and parishes is naive at best and dishonest at worst. Jesus needed his disciples, despite their fear, to go with him to Jerusalem. We need one another for a similar journey.

Prayer

God of Us,
We are a becoming people. Be patient with us as our hearts seek you. You are our treasure. Like Vera, open our arms for welcoming after-school hugs. Spend time with us, and listen with compassion to our stories. Sustain us as we try to do the same with others. Bring us to a heart place, God of Relationships, where we can see and sort our priorities. Help us to replace I and me with we and us. May our lifestyle reflect gospel values as we become a sign of your presence in the world. Amen.

Doorway Reflections

- What centers and prepares you to be more present to others?
- What lifestyle is God calling you to live?
- Where do you find peace and contentment in your life?
- Name your priorities. What and where is your treasure?
- Choose a symbol that reflects where your heart is.
- What questions, challenges, possibilities do Vera and Don offer us? Is change or recommitment needed?
- How is your family a community of faith?

A Doorway of Surprise

Be still, and know that I am God!
(Ps 46:10)

Living in the inner city has always been different. The first time I moved from New York City to New Hampshire, I couldn't sleep for a few days. Not enough noise at night. Now that I have moved back to inner-city Boston, a new phenomenon is offering me many opportunities to pray.

Each morning I walk around our neighborhood for a half hour or so. Being a bit compulsive, I usually walk at the same time each morning, which means I meet the same people on my route. One teenager is especially friendly. Perhaps because he sees my white hair, he bows slightly, smiles, and encourages me, saying, "Almost home." I smile, keep moving, and wonder if I actually look like I am about to collapse.

Then there is Tony, the screamer. Obviously mentally ill, Tony sometimes walks our streets without shoes or proper clothes. But most days he stands on the last step of his apartment building and greets each passerby, even those only a few feet away, with a very loud shout. Determined to get to know him a little bit, I stopped last fall and tried to engage him in conversation. He smiled pleasantly at my inquiry but continued to shout about whatever was on his mind. Nothing seemed to get through to him. I left, and tried again the next day. Still no response. Then for several weeks I simply walked by and waved as Tony shouted.

After a brief trip to Nevada for a conference, I came home and took my morning walk, but no Tony. After three days, I was worried. Where could he be? Was he all right? I asked our local pastor if he had seen him. And then I realized that I missed

Tony. That he was an occasion of prayer for me. Not only had I smiled at him each morning and said hello, I prayed for him, his family, our neighborhood, and all the mentally ill. Tony was like the churches of my youth. You never passed by without making the sign of the cross and whispering a prayer or two. And just like the churches of my youth, he is no longer around.

Many years ago, Catherine de Hueck Doherty wrote that we need to make a corner of our heart into a Poustinia, a desert place where we can know God intimately despite all that is happening around us. That is what Tony often reminded me to do. As far as I know no one enters Tony's heart easily. I can only imagine his shouting as a way of challenging all who ignore him to listen to the person behind the yelling. We might even discover a holy man. Be surprised, his shouting suggests. God is trying to speak.

Children seem to know this more easily than adults. Don't our little ones often sneak off by themselves to quiet places for play, especially when their lives get too cluttered? And didn't Jesus go into the desert immediately after being baptized by John? Transformed, he needed time to think, pray, and breathe. Both shouting Tony and Jesus remind all to be quiet, to pray always, and to be grateful each day for the gift of God's unconditional love.

Prayer

God of all Corners and Surprises,
Make me awake to the Tonys of my life, all those occasions of
prayer. Surprise me by your people on all my morning walks. Open
my heart to welcome them. Lead me into a corner of my heart, my
Poustinia, my desert place where you dwell. Let me hear the inti-
macy of your whispering voice: "Be still and know that I am God.

Be still and know that I am. Be still and know. Be still. Be." Quiet my being, still my heart, as I slowly let go of your words until there is only "be." Amen.

Doorway Reflections

- How do others see you on your walks of life?
- What is an occasion of prayer for you?
- Like Tony, who are your churches today where you whisper a prayer as you pass by? Whom do you welcome into your heart? To whom or for what do you close your heart?
- How do you listen beyond the shouting of your outside and inside world? Where are your quiet places?
- What is the feel and place of your Poustinia where you know God intimately?

 # A Listening Place

Come to me, all you that are weary and are carrying heavy burdens, and I will give you rest. (Matt 11:28)

"I've been unhappy, Mike," Sheila said one night to her husband as they were getting ready for bed. Mike said nothing. "Are you listening, Michael?" Sheila asked. Finally, Mike answered, "I heard you, Sheila. I'm just not sure how to respond. I'm very tired. It's been a long day and I would rather talk in the morning."

"Mike," Sheila said, "the mornings are so rushed. I just don't think there will be time. If you can't answer right away that's okay, but listen to me. Please."

"Okay," Mike said, as he turned to face his wife. "I'm listening."

"Jeremy is very quiet these days. His teachers tell me that his schoolwork has fallen off badly. He comes home and heads straight for the computer. I only let him use it for half an hour but even then he just shrugs and mopes around the house. He tells me he did all his homework in school."

Mike said nothing for a while. Finally, trying hard to be gentle, Mike said, "Jeremy is twelve, Sheila. He's growing, changing. He'll be okay."

"It's not Jeremy who is making me unhappy, Mike. It's you, or rather, your relationship with Jeremy. You walk in the house, pick up the mail, ask about phone calls, and hide behind the newspaper until supper is ready. You used to have a catch with Jeremy when you came home. Ask about his homework. Now you don't ask about anyone, including me." Mike breathed deeply, tempted to defend himself, to offer an explanation. Rather, he admitted, "Jeremy confuses me, Sheila. I dreamed about having a son for so long. Now he seems very distant from me. I want to believe that it is nothing. But it bothers me. How do you talk to a twelve-year-old?"

Now it was Sheila's turn to breathe. "Thank you," she said. "Thank you. I am so glad to hear you say that. I was so worried it was just me Jeremy couldn't stand."

If we hope to find the courage to begin again, reconciliation has to happen first at home, even in the bedroom if that is the place where we talk about intimate matters. The rite of reconciliation reminds us that "the church is good but in need of purification" (Rite of Penance #3). In other words, unless we acknowledge our faults, at home first of all, we will be unable to remember our goodness and find reconciliation and renewal.

Jesus says it this way: "Come to me, all you that are weary and are carrying heavy burdens, and I will give you rest" (Matt 11:28).

Parenting often brings great challenges. Being a mother or father to five-year-olds is very different from parenting teenagers. Nevertheless, faith tells us that when we take time to think, reflect, pray, and speak about the changes that face all of us so frequently, we not only avoid unnecessary arguments, we honor ourselves, our families, and our God at the same time.

Prayer

God of Listening Places,

Too busy, tired, heavy burdened, preoccupied with my own agenda, I am sometimes unaware of what is happening around me. Unlike you, Listening God, I am often not available to the people I love. Give me courage to acknowledge my absenteeism and, like Mike, overcome my temptation to defend myself by making excuses. Bid me through others to start over, to reconcile and walk together again. With another lead me to a listening place to rest, forgive, and remember the goodness of all people in you. Amen.

Doorway Reflections

- How do you provide a safe, welcoming place for sharing your concerns?
- How do you listen and talk with another about your concerns? When and how do you have difficulty finding a listening place? Who listens to your struggles?
- To whom do you offer a listening presence? When, where, and how do you speak of intimate matters and take time to reflect and attend to changes in your life?

- What are the difficulties you experience in your family and community? With whom do you struggle? How do you reconcile?

 ## Barroom Doors

Teach me your way, O LORD,
and lead me on a level path. (Ps 27:11)

Timid and unsure, Carl was searching desperately for meaning in his life. As a young boy, he had entertained the idea of becoming a priest, but his embarrassment in front of his friends and the new experience of his attraction to girls soon dissuaded him. By the time he was sixteen, he had rejected the idea of confirmation and had not seen the inside of a church for three years.

In the beginning of his alienation Carl told himself that he was too busy to go to church. Two jobs, baseball practice, and the lure of long Sunday morning sleeps made it easy for him to avoid church. For a while, his parents insisted on his attendance, but after many fruitless and acrimonious quarrels, they decided not to push further.

At twenty, Carl fell in love with a gentle young woman. Sure that he had found his soul mate, he was devastated when Liz told him their relationship was not working for her. How could he have missed the signals that their love would not last? For a while, Carl wandered through life and a series of short relationships. No longer sure what he wanted to be or do, he experimented with drugs, often drank too much, and even occasionally found himself thinking about military service.

Someplace inside himself he knew he was running, without direction or purpose.

Enter Matt, the assistant youth minister at his old parish church. They had been fast friends in grammar school. Matt and Carl ran into each other at a summer softball game. Afterward they went out for a beer and began talking. Soon the conversation turned toward what they were doing with their lives. When Matt told Carl about his church involvement, Carl feigned indifference but was intrigued. What motivated Matt to go into church work? What kept him working at a job that paid so poorly? Did he really believe everything they had learned as children?

Matt anticipated Carl's last question. "The church really has changed a lot, Carl. Give me a call, I'd love to tell you all about us." The next day, unable to get his mind off their conversation and intrigued by Matt's use of the word *us*, Carl called Matt and told him that he was going to church that Sunday and would love to talk with him afterward.

Though bars are sometimes places where serious disease emerges, they can also be safe places where people talk easily about important matters. When Carl and Matt walked through the barroom door together, Carl's life changed radically, but so did Matt's. While Carl was searching for new meaning in his life, Matt also had to face questions to which there were no easy answers.

Robert Frost, in "The Road Not Taken," reminds us that life often has strange twists to which we must respond. Challenging us to take the less traveled road, Frost confronts us in much the same way as Jesus who says, "If any want to become my followers, let them deny themselves and take up their cross daily and follow me" (Luke 9:23). The invitation to walk with another along the dark roads of life, helping to carry his or her cross, is a great privilege. Take a moment to be grateful for everyone who has ever listened to your story, and for the gift of listening to others.

Prayer

God of We and Us,
Timid and unsure, indifferent and intrigued, we search for meaning with others. You call us to travel known and unknown paths. Protect the way. Lighten our traveling feet. Guide and direct our restless spirits. Answer the needs of our searching hearts. Make safe all the roads of life. And make our journey your journey, God of We and Us. Amen.

Doorway Reflections

- What motivates you in your work?
- Are you more like Carl, searching for new meaning, or like Matt, facing questions with no easy answers, or like the prodigal son, finally "coming to your senses" and going home?
- Where are the barrooms of your life?
- Are you more likely to choose a worn and traveled path, or make your own as you go?
- What are you doing with your life?
- Think of the last time you had to make a choice in your direction in life. Was it easy? Hard? What path or person made all of the difference?

Doorways of Compassion

Lost,
like a child in a mall,
a teenager in a changing body,
a wife abandoned by her husband,
or a grandmother whose children never visit,
we are not alone.
God is a shepherd, a beacon, a refuge,
who cannot stop looking for us.

Compassion is one of the attributes of God that both calms and challenges us. That God is compassionate is clear. God listens to the cries of his people in Egypt and in the desert, on stormy seas and in abandoned villages, in the midst of wars and in everyday life. God listens and does not judge harshly. God walks with and never abandons us. As the prophet Isaiah reminds us:

> Can a woman forget her nursing child,
>   or show no compassion for the child of her womb?
> Even these may forget,
>   yet I will not forget you. (Isa 49:15)

But God as compassionate mother also challenges us. We cannot, in justice, forget the hungry, imprisoned, homeless, and sick. In fact, Matthew insists, we are to treat all as if they were the

Christ. "Just as you did it to one of the least of these who are members of my family, you did it to me" (Matt 25:40).

The following reflections are about compassion in its fullest sense. When we look with kindness on others who are struggling, when we put aside all temptation to judge those who are broken, when we see those with nothing and remember our own nothingness, we are compassionate.

Every day, we insist, there are opportunities to witness and to give witness to a gospel life. In every town and village, indeed, in every neighborhood there are heroes and heroines of God—people who never stop offering themselves as "safe shelter" for those who are lost or who have been abandoned. They are the saints all around us and as *Doorways of Compassion*, even in our darkest days, they fill us with new hope.

Doorways of Standing

I can do all things through him who strengthens me. (Phil 4:13)

Sister David has been a Poor Clare more than fifty years. She is lively, outgoing, and always kind, and everyone loves her, especially children. An extern sister who does much of the community shopping, she also goes to dozens of funerals and formal church events as a representative of her community. She is the face of the Poor Clares in Boston.

But she is getting tired. Her back is chronically inflamed and she has a hard time standing up after she sits down. Recently, she told me that she eats two of her three daily meals standing up in order not to struggle with her weakening legs. "But that's all right," she said. "If that is all God asks, I'll be fine." I smiled as I listened to her. Her gratitude is overwhelming. Even her struggles to sit and walk do not get in the way of her serving everyone she meets and being grateful for the everyday gifts of life and faith.

Recently, I was telling nine-year-old Maggie about Sister David standing for two meals every day. Maggie smiled, then frowned, and wandered away. That evening I noticed Maggie was not sitting in her regular seat at her grandma's picnic table. Holding her food carefully, she was standing talking to her younger brother. Easing my way over to her, I asked her if she would like to sit down. "No," she said, "I was thinking of your friend, Sister David, and this is my prayer for her. No one should be alone when they eat." I nodded, picked up my food, and stood next to Maggie, much like the Jews eating the first Passover meal (Exod 12), waiting for the Lord to set them free.

Children hear everything. Though not always able to act on what they hear, they sometimes amaze us with their compassion and understanding. Perhaps that is why Jesus put a little child in front of a crowd with whom he was speaking and said, "Truly I tell you, unless you change and become like children, you will never enter the kingdom of heaven" (Matt 18:3–4). Maggie asked me to change by her simple gesture of solidarity and taught me an entirely new way of being present to my friend Sister David. Now, whenever I am standing for a long time, I think of Sister David, of her acceptance of aging and her enduring gratitude for all God's gifts.

Solidarity with and care for the aging comes naturally to most children. Perhaps because they identify with the vulnerability of older people, children are very comfortable around them, speaking naturally and effortlessly about their simple fears and joys. And because the elderly listen, children are not quick to leave them to search for other friends. Their shared needs bond them together. We are on a journey, children and older people teach us, and when we stand and walk together in solidarity, it is very short.

Prayer

God of All Standings,
I am awed by the sensitivity of young Maggie and long to pray her standing meal prayer. I fail so often to welcome your presence in this gesture, Standing God. I struggle to be attentive and available to your Spirit for others. I want to be more like standing Maggie, O God, in solidarity with all your people.

We are one in you and in you all is sacred. This is my prayer, a yes to oneness, to solidarity with people and creation. Help me to be open, like Maggie, to receiving those people or circumstances given me by you. Give me space to allow your prayer to be prayed in me for them. And let me hear your prayer for me as we stand together, God. Amen.

Doorway Reflections

- For what everyday gifts are you grateful?
- Like Maggie's standing prayer for Sister David, what and for whom is your prayer of solidarity?
- At this time in your life, how do you experience God's prayer for you?
- Who asks you to change by a simple gesture?
- Reflect on your own experience of aging and diminishment and the way you serve out of it.
- With whom and how do you "speak naturally and effortlessly about your fears and joy"?

- What has a child or older person taught you?
- Who stands with you in your faith journey? What shared needs bond you together? Ask God: For whom and how would you have me pray for this person?

Lost Doorways

I am the good shepherd...And I lay down my life for the sheep. (John 10:13, 15)

Distracted by a difficult conversation with an old friend, I almost bumped into an older gentleman as I left the local coffeeshop. "Excuse me," he said. "I'm a little turned around and seem to have lost my way. Could you point me toward Ossining?"

"Sure," I said, "but that's five miles away. Are you walking?"

"Well, I came by bus, all right, but I can't remember which one. So I thought I'd walk home. I have my address right here on my health insurance card. I'll find my way."

Looking at the address, I knew immediately that this older man would not be able to walk. "Wait right here," I said. "I'm going toward Ossining and I'll give you a ride."

"Thanks," he said. "If that isn't too much trouble, I'd be very grateful."

"By the way," I asked, "what's your name?"

"Joe," he said, "Joe Abraham. Both names are in the Bible. Makes it easy to remember." I smiled and left to get my car.

A few minutes later, I picked Joe up and headed for Ossining. Not sure exactly where he lived, I asked him if he knew how to get home. Joe hesitated. "It's near the center of town, I can walk from there." Everything in me knew that I could not drop Joe off in the middle of town. "Let's try to find your house," I said. "It will be an adventure and will help me learn my way around Ossining." Half an hour later, still lost, I stopped at a service station to ask for help. A few minutes later we pulled up to Joe's home.

Getting out of the car Joe turned to me and said, "Will it always be this way?"

I hesitated, not wanting to hurt or frighten him. "Yes," I said, "you are going to have to be very careful. It is easy to get lost."

"Right," he said, "and thanks. I'll try to be more careful."

Driving away from Joe's home I was near tears. What must it be like to lose one's memory? To be lost whenever one gets a short distance from home? Joe's dilemma got me thinking about my own journey. How many times have I asked God: "Will it always be this way?" Hoping for a comforting answer, I knew that all of us have to take life on its terms. We don't make the rules and must live as best we can with the gifts we have and the faults we carry. I wished it were different for me, for Joe, for us, but I knew it wasn't. Despite making me very late for an appointment, Joe helped me pray and I was grateful for our encounter and journey.

It is not only the elderly who lose their way. All of us, especially our children, often get lost inside our fears, doubts, and resentments and find it almost impossible to find our way without help. Our task is clear. Without being patronizing or judgmental, we need to accompany one another in faith, especially when we are lost. The divorced, separated, grieving, and addicted, to name just a few, often feel painfully lost. But like Joe, they can be a gift to us when they accept that "it will always be this way." Their admission challenges us to do the same. And when we accept that we are lost, we discover that God, like a Good Shepherd, is willing to be lost with us.

Prayer

God of the Lost,
I'm a little turned around again. I've lost my sense of direction and
I yearn to come home to you. The lyrics of an old song haunt me:
"Show me the way to go home, I'm tired." It's so easy to be lost,
weary, tired, fear-filled, lonely. With Joe Abraham I ask you, "Will it
always be this way?" And I can hear your gentle whisper, "Yes, yes,
but you are not alone. I love being lost with you." Help me to accept
and carry both my gifts and faults. Be my Good Shepherd.
Accompany me. Let me find my home in you. Amen.

Doorway Reflections

- Who accompanies you when you are a "little turned around"?
- In what fears, doubts, or resentments do you sometimes find yourself lost? How do you accept being lost?
- When and where is it difficult to admit your need for help?
- Recall an experience like the meeting with Joe Abraham that helped you pray.

 # Doorways of Joy

I have said these things to you so that my
joy may be in you, and that your joy may be
complete. (John 15:11)

Quiet, reflective, and sensitive, Claire's heart had always challenged her to think about and do something for others, especially the very poor. Soup kitchens and community closets helped feed her need but she knew that before she married, she wanted to spend time outside her own culture, working alongside the poor, especially poor women. When the possibility of spending a year in Honduras emerged, she jumped at the chance. And that year changed her life.

Because Claire's Spanish was rudimentary at best, she had to become even quieter. Listening without understanding very much became a metaphor that helped her understand her entire life more completely. As she struggled to pay attention to conversations among the women alongside whom she worked, she realized that in not understanding their rapid Spanish, she was becoming very reflective about all the conversations she had missed in English because she answered too quickly or found them uninteresting or shallow.

At the same time, her quiet, reflective listening began to pay big dividends. The women of Ocotepeque, Honduras, started to confide in her. Not only did they speak of their dreams and hopes, especially for their children, they also shared their fears and anxieties about husbands who drank too much and became violent toward them and their children. Because Claire could only listen, nod, and occasionally cry with them, the women of Ocotepeque saw her as a friend and companion who not only would not but could not speak about the confidences they shared. Claire was like a sponge. She took everything in and held it gently. In truth, she could do nothing else. Ironically, though Claire ached to speak Spanish more fluently, her listening presence was exactly what her new friends wanted and needed.

Now, fourteen years later, Claire is a mother of three and an artist, and Honduras, especially its women, will not leave her memory. When she sold her first pots, plates, and bowls, she was overwhelmed by the words and attitudes of those who saw her work. "Beautiful," they whispered, and "wonderful. I wish there was more I could buy." And because she had also exhibited and sold her children's creations, Claire knew their joy would not be complete until they shared their bounty with the women of Honduras. I was not surprised when I received a check for half the amount she realized from the sale of her art.

Among the first virtues to which our religious tradition challenges us are awe and wonder. We are to stand quietly in the midst of all creation and praise God with joy for all God's gifts. No doubt Claire learned this lesson as a child growing up along the Hudson River, but she relearned it in Honduras. Our children know it instinctively. As we listen to their "ahs" when viewing a sunset, a fireworks display, or a deer by the side of the road, we know that God is in them, changing them. Like the Jewish people in the desert, grateful for all God's gifts, they cry out,

> Who is like you, O LORD, among the gods?
> Who is like you, majestic in holiness,
> awesome in splendor, doing wonders? (Exod 15:11)

Surely, these same sentiments were in Claire's heart when she ministered in Honduras. No doubt they are even more deeply embedded in ours when we hear of her generosity.

Prayer

God of All Joy and Wonder,
We praise you for gifts great and small. You are our Wonder-
Maker. Open our eyes and ears to the splendor of your people and
all of creation. Like the Claires of our world, give us hands and
hearts that work alongside the poor, listening to their stories, being

present to their hopes and fears. May our joy be complete in you and in our shared life of generosity. Gracious, generous God, thank you. Amen.

Doorway Reflections

- When do you become reflective in your listening?
- Who shares their dreams, hopes, fears, and anxieties with you?
- What do you hold gently in your heart that continues to nurture you in your ministry?
- Compose and share a list of "ahs" in your life right now.
- How do you experience God's joy in you? Take a moment to listen to God's prayer for you.

Doorways of Visitation

In him we live and move and have our being. (Acts 17:28)

After I anointed two people in a local hospital for the indigent, a woman was waiting for me in the corridor. Painfully thin and missing a leg, she sat in a wheelchair blocking my exit. Looking directly at me, she asked, "Do you visit people?" "Yes," I said. "Would you visit me?" she asked. "Of course," I said. And with a sweeping gesture, Awina invited me into her room. Struck by the room's careful arrangement and neat appearance, I suggested to Awina that she must have a good relationship with the maintenance staff to have such a clean and neat room. "Well," she said, "this is the first time I have ever had my own place. I keep it neat like this. Right now it is all I have."

Then Awina told me her story. After her mother died when she was five years old, she lived with her father, who abandoned her at seven. Sent to live with an aunt, Awina was addicted to drugs at fourteen, and had a child at sixteen. Homeless at seventeen, she moved around New York City for years. Finally acknowledging how desperate her life had become, Awina came to Massachusetts to live with her daughter, but her addiction was still raging. Within three months Awina was homeless again.

One evening Awina awoke on the street surrounded by police. At first she thought she had killed someone, but the police assured her they only wanted to take her to a hospital because her leg was badly infected. Not sure if she was hallucinating, Awina remembers telling the doctors to remove her leg if that would keep her alive. Then, looking up and directly at me, but without a word about her missing leg, Awina said, "This is my last chance. Will you pray with me?"

Where does hope like this come from? How do people like Awina manage to see a future when almost all their memories are dark? Awina herself gives us the answer. "Will you pray with me?" she begs. Having the faith to pray is pure gift, not something we earn or deserve, but the ongoing action of God within us and our communities. It is the realization that, despite our faults and sins, we are God's children. As Douglas Steer suggests, "We not only pray for each other but suffer for each other." Like a seed, faith grows in us, sometimes like a wild flower. Blooming in the middle of an empty lot littered with broken liquor bottles, it gives us hope despite our losses and failures.

Awina's life, newly hope-filled despite the loss of her leg, is a challenge to us. Are we cultivating the seed of faith within us? Are we praying regularly, gathering with other believers for the breaking of the bread, reaching out to those who have no one?

More, are we willing to be stopped and touched by those with nothing? Awina was and is a blessing to us, a reminder that God is never very far, in fact, is often blocking the hallways of our lives when we want only to flee. God is fiercely loyal, indefatigable, unable not to love us. We have only to stand still.

Prayer

God of a Thousand Chances,
You are our life—"we live, move, and have our being in you."
Sometimes like wild flowers growing in an empty lot of losses and
failures, we plead for hope. We are weak, afraid, alone. Cultivate
the seed of faith within us. Let Awina lead us to a future beyond
our dark memories. And send us, Indefatigable God, to be stopped
and touched by those with nothing. Block the hallways of our lives
when we want to flee from the nearness of your presence in the
homeless and addicted. Make us visitors of your people. Amen.

Doorway Reflections

- Who has invited you to visit them? How are you present at these visitations? How do you pray with others and not just for them?
- Reflect on all you have right now. How is this a blessing or a woe?
- Like Awina, who anoints you by their stories?
- When has your life been desperate? Who was there for you?
- When you stand still, what is your name for the nearness of God in your life?

The Good News Door

Go into all the world and proclaim the good news to the whole creation. (Mark 16:15)

Tall, thin, centered, and quiet, Megan has been helping coordinate our third-grade family program for several years. Though very skilled as a facilitator and group leader, she rarely inserts herself into the dynamics of our group process unless it is clearly necessary. In other words, Megan is the kind of woman every director of religious education dreams about when assembling a team to form children in faith.

In the middle of the sexual abuse scandal, when our parish was hit especially hard, Megan remained calm and helpful but reserved. Despite being a child life expert, she chose not to act in this capacity in our program. One Sunday, however, when I was speaking about compassion as an essential virtue for Christians and families, I paused to ask if people needed to speak about the crisis in our church as it was affecting their children. When several people nodded affirmatively, I invited Megan to respond to the questions of the parents.

Without hesitation and with immense grace, Megan listened to the inquiries of our parents and assured them that she had already spoken with her own children about how to respond to inappropriate touches or advances. As she spoke, a deep calm came upon the room. It was not only her expertise that helped those present, it was her tone and attitude. There were no silly or poor questions, she assured us, and we ought to ask every question that might help protect our children. Though the crisis was not going to disappear quickly, if we attended to our children's needs gently and listened to them carefully, they would "catch" our love and be fine.

Jesus often spoke like this in the Gospels. In fact, his words were so "full of authority" that his listeners asked: "Where did he get all this?" At the same time, Jesus did not cling to his power but shared it with us. "Receive the Holy Spirit,…and…go to all nations," proclaiming good news. The proclamation of faith is an effort of the entire Church. It is not something reserved for the clergy and religious. The Second Vatican Council's *Dogmatic Constitution on the Church* states that "these faithful are by baptism made one body with Christ and are established among the People of God….They carry out their own part in the mission of the whole Christian people with respect to the Church and the world" (§ 31).

In recent years, every diocese and parish we know employs skilled laypeople to help foster faith and give leadership and direction to the Church. At the same time, the age of the laity has only begun. As more and more people like Megan surface and demonstrate their abilities to lead, we will have to empower them with the authority they need to give focus to their skills.

More important, people like Megan are everywhere. In fact, there are more lay theologians and catechists now than at any time in the Church's history. As we accept the challenge of reshaping the Church in the third millennium, it would be tragic not to employ the skills, wisdom, and insights of qualified laypeople. Our children deserve the best we can offer them in education and religious formation. Let us pray for the humility to extend our hand of need to all who can help heal us.

Prayer

God of All Good News,
We are church. Let us become and recognize what we already are,
your presence in the world. Give us the immense grace of a Megan
to be there for others in troubled and confusing times as we listen
carefully and attend gently to the needs of others. Use us to protect
and guide your little ones. As church empower us to lead, proclaim,
and be your good news in the world today. Amen.

Doorway Reflections

- How are you church, a sign of God's love and care to others?
- Like Megan, when have you communicated by your tone and attitude more than your expertise?
- How do you speak with children about how to respond to inappropriate touches and advances?
- In what ways are you a door of good news in proclaiming your faith?
- Who has supported and empowered you to be a leader in your church?

# Doorways of Touch

A woman who had been suffering from
hemorrhages for twelve years came up
behind him and touched the fringe of his
cloak, for she said to herself, "If I only touch
his cloak, I will be made well."
(Matt 9:20–21)

Peg and Bill were always beautiful. Alive, engaged, and faith-filled, they were a happy and vibrant couple. Active in civic and church affairs, one could always call them for help or just a word of encouragement. Their love for life and one another was tangible. Nothing seemed able to blunt their enthusiasm and generosity. Even the numbing motorcycle accident of their sixteen-year-old son, Timmy, seemed unable to break their spirit. In a coma, and on life support systems for weeks, Tim had serious brain damage when he finally awoke. Still Peg and Bill remained positive and with the support of friends and their deep faith, they found a path through their terrible darkness. Until Peg's illness.

Peg had been coughing for weeks and nothing seemed to give her relief for very long. What first seemed like a bad cold, and then a serious infection, soon became life threatening. Bill called late one night. Peg had been taken to the hospital and was in intensive care. Her doctors were worried that her lung damage was irreversible.

When I first visited, Peg was under heavy sedation. I called Bill and he was near panic, telling me that the doctors were going to put Peg on a ventilator to help her breathe but were not very positive about her chances for survival. Weeks went by and although Peg clung to life, she was often unable to respond to my visits at all. Though I prayed, held her hand, and encouraged her to keep fighting, I wondered if she was hearing or feeling anything I said or did.

One night I called Bill to see how he was doing. "I'm fine, Gaynell, and Peg is going to be fine too. Today I was able to kiss her on the lips for the first time in weeks and that is always the way we got through the hard times. I know now she is going to be all right." Listening to Bill's faith and hope brought me near tears. Bill reminded me of the woman in the gospel, bleeding for years, who wanted only to touch the hem of the Lord's robe in order to get well.

The gospel is alive and strong in so many hearts and lives. And our children often seem able to see this more easily than we can. Almost every Sunday night when we gather for a family dinner my grandchildren startle me with the directness and honesty of their prayers. Several years after the destruction of the World Trade Center, Maggie still prays for the children whose parents died that day. And her younger brother Peter never fails to remind us that too many children don't have enough food. These little ones remind us to have the same faith and hope of the bleeding woman and Bill. Because they have learned to pray now, I have no doubt that they will remember to kiss their spouses and children when they get older. Kissing is a wonderful prayer.

Prayer

Close your eyes...Pay attention to your breath...Breath is spirit, life...God blew into us the breath of life...Note your breath...Watch it...Follow it...In and out...Fill your abdomen with God's breath of life, the supreme gift. Inhale all that is of God, and exhale all that seems not to be of God. While you continue slowing your breath, begin your breath prayer: inhale and hear the word touch; *exhale and hear the words* be healed. *Keep repeating these words to yourself in silence.*

Doorway Reflections

- Like Peg and Bill, who are the people of your life who live in faith and hope? Tell and pray their story.
- When have you needed to touch the hem of Jesus' cloak? Who has wrapped you in a cloak of healing by their listening

presence? How do you breathe through the difficult dark times of life? With whom do you gather weekly for a Sabbath dinner? What are the prayers of the children in your life? Do you know the joy of kissing as a prayer?

A Braided Doorway

For, in fact, the kingdom of God is among you. (Luke 17:21)

Bored with myself and the world, I knew I needed a fix. Tempted to loaf or go to the movies, I decided instead to get out of my own way and visit a local homeless shelter. St. Francis House in downtown Boston is a remarkable place. Started by the Franciscan Friars, it is now run by a group of deeply caring laypeople who provide a wide variety of services to Boston's homeless and hungry. St. Francis House provides not only nutritious meals and a community closet, but also dozens of twelve-step meetings, group and individual counseling sessions, and hot showers for those who simply want to clean up.

Wandering through the day room, I watched as the homeless socialized. Some chatted quietly, others played cards, and many dozed, but in the center of this very crowded room a young woman was braiding hair. I knew Lucretia. Tough and direct, she was also full of compassion. Once homeless herself, she knew how much she missed simple touch when she was on the streets. Demanding only that the homeless first shower or bathe, Lucretia braids their hair and provides them and herself with a sense of dignity that homelessness often steals. The patience that Lucretia showed and the stillness that came over the man whose hair she was braiding fascinated me. I had to keep myself from staring. Or crying.

St. Francis of Assisi tells his followers that the thought of getting close to lepers as a young man "was turned into sweetness of body and soul" when the Lord led him to kiss a leper. Graced to reach past and beyond his fears and reluctance, St. Francis realized that the leper was a symbol for all that was wrong with his life and world. By kissing the leper, St. Francis discovered in the face of all those whom society rejects an image of Christ on the cross and that led him to fall in love with all the throwaway people in his time.

Our children need to meet people like Lucretia and to hear about others like St. Francis. These saints will shake them out of any complacency or insensitivity contemporary society might foster. Moreover, children who are exposed early to those in real need almost always become sensitized to the plight of poor people for the rest of their lives. Because they meet the poor as persons and not as a social class, they have no prejudices about them.

In fact, children who meet the poor in soup kitchens and community pantries regularly ask their parents why some people have to live with so little hope. Because we have no easy answers, we are forced to think more deeply about social justice. Lucretia, St. Francis, and our children, without ever intending it or realizing it, help us see the face of Christ in people and places where we rarely look. More important, they help us realize that living a gospel life is not first of all about being bright or insightful but about doing the simplest of actions with care and concern. Braiding a person's hair, when done with compassion and love, is a powerful work of mercy that will change not only the people directly involved, but all who witness it.

Prayer

Creator Spirit,
Braid my hair. Through your touch, release in me compassion for
the homeless parts of myself and others. Let me feel your tears of
compassion. Every work of love brings me face to face with you.
Expand my heart in serving others, so they can believe in them-
selves again. Instill in my heart the daily prayer of Cardinal
Newman: "Make me preach you without preaching, not by words
but by my example, by the catching force, the sympathetic influ-
ence of what I do…the evident fullness of the love that my heart
bears to you." Amen.

Doorway Reflections

- What do you do to get out of your own way?
- What are the resistances to the homeless parts of yourself?
- Where do you see, as Mother Teresa did, Jesus in the "distress-ing disguise of the poor"? Who are our culture's throwaway people?
- Wander through a day in your life and revisit the acts of com-passion you witness.
- Name and pray in gratitude for those people in your life who are like St. Francis and Lucretia.

A Mending Door

Morning by morning he wakens—
wakens my ear to listen as those who are
taught. (Isa 50:4)

Sarah had always been a sensitive child. In first grade she regularly came home upset because some children were treated badly not just by other students but by teachers. No wonder she reacted so powerfully and quickly to the attack on the World Trade Center. Three days after the tragedy she organized the children in her neighborhood. With her younger brother Peter and sister Maggie in charge of the design of their booth, she and two classmates set about creating a sign they could affix to cardboard. Surrounded by dozens of pictures of firefighters and police digging and walking into burning buildings, the sign read: "Peace is not the opposite of war, creation is. Help us help the rescuers."

Like many children, Sarah has a tender and intimate relationship with the earth. She loves to kneel in the garden next to her grandmother, pull weeds, plant new flowers, and talk about life as she experiences it. The World Trade Center disaster was not just the collapse of a building and the death of thousands of people, it polluted the air, destroyed the earth below it, and shattered her picture of what life is supposed to be.

Children like Sarah have the ability to help us change in fundamental ways. While many adults, trying to understand terrorism, react to the event itself by vowing vengeance, children move on, not to vindictiveness but to reconciliation and rebuilding. Sarah and her friends challenge us to see bigger pictures and find a faith response not only to the horror of September 11, 2001, but to a different way of living in the world. For them, the only authentic response to destruction is to rebuild, to create anew, to restore the earth.

Pope John Paul II had a similar response shortly after the destruction of the World Trade Center the attack on the Pentagon, and the crash of the plane in Pennsylvania. Decrying the wanton taking of so many innocent lives, the Holy Father reminded the world that the ground in which terrorism is planted is ignorance, poverty, and hunger. Unless we find ways to reconcile people across cultures, races, and religions by addressing major human rights issues, terrorism and other forms of violence will surely continue.

Jesus challenged us with much the same message at the end of Matthew's Gospel: "For I was hungry and you gave me food, I was thirsty and you gave me something to drink…Then the righteous will answer him, 'Lord, when was it that we saw you hungry and gave you food, or thirsty and gave you something to drink?'…'Truly I tell you, just as you did it to one of the least of these who are members of my family, you did it to me'" (Matt 25:35, 37, 40). Feeding the hungry and clothing the naked is a much more compelling witness to the truth of our convictions than any argument. Sarah and her friends, trying to help those most in need and the earth itself, lived the truth of Jesus by restoring the damage done to the earth. We pray for the courage to follow their example.

Prayer

Creator God,
You are the Maker of all that is good. You delight in the handiwork
of your creation. But now our world seems topsy turvy. Give us hope
in walking hand in hand as brothers and sisters to rebuild, replant,
reconcile, begin, and create anew. Give us a "yes" to each day, a lis-
tening heart to each moment. Be with us in the morning as we stand
with hands open to accept all that lies ahead, and in the evening
with hands open and now extended, handing over to you, Mending
God, all that has happened. Amen.

Doorway Reflections

- Where were you and what were you doing when you heard the news of September 11, 2001? What were or are your feelings?
- What people did you talk with? What is something you heard in the conversation or read that gave you hope? Has any Scripture passage or story been helpful for you?
- Reflect on the response of Sarah and her friends and their words: "Peace is not the opposite of war, creation is. Help us help the rescuers." How would you respond to John Paul II's call to reconcile people across cultures, races, religions?

Doors of Justice

What does the LORD require of you
but to do justice, and to love kindness,
and to walk humbly with your God?
(Mic 6:8)

Fifteen and ferocious. That's how Caitlin's dad Damien described her. Committed to helping create a more just world, Caitlin joined Greenpeace, Pax Christi USA, and the Living Wage movement, and directed her youth group's attempt to bring leftover food from the school cafeteria to a local soup kitchen. Formed and shaped by both her parents, Caitlin had a very tender conscience that her parents admired and feared at the same time. Not only did she understand the world's failure to distribute food and land more justly, she felt it. It was no surprise, then, when Caitlin told her parents that her private Catholic high school education was too expensive. She wanted to talk with them about going to the local public school and diverting her tuition money to people and projects who provided direct service to the poor.

Caitlin's parents were troubled by her request. Their daughter's school gave her access not just to projects that fostered justice but to the literature and history that grounded her dreams in the best of the Catholic tradition. Though they were both college graduates, they did not feel competent to educate her further in the social teaching of the Church that would ready her for life in the twenty-first century. But Caitlin insisted that she could find groups that would help her reflect carefully outside her school environment. Damien asked his daughter whether she was unhappy in high school or if something had happened to upset her. When Caitlin denied difficulty in school, her parents felt stumped. What could they do; what should they do?

Megan McKenna tells the story of the farmer who visited New York City to meet a businessman and sell his crop. The businessman, hoping to impress the farmer, took him to lunch in the bedlam of New York at noon. Surrounded by thousands of people scurrying about, the farmer said, "Shhhh...I think I hear a cricket." The businessman smiled smugly and suggested that even if there was a cricket to be found in New York City, the farmer couldn't possibly hear it. With that, the farmer walked to an outdoor flower pot, turned over a fallen leaf, and picked up a cricket. Impressed, the businessman asked the farmer how he heard the cricket. The farmer smiled slyly, stopped again, put his hand in his pocket, took out a fistful of coins, and dropped them on the sidewalk. Many people heard the tinkle of the coins and started to pick them up. Watching the frenetic search, the farmer said, "The heart hears what moves it."

Though we may not know exactly how to react to Caitlin's sensitivity, we can have no doubt what Jesus means when he says: "Do not store up for yourselves treasures on earth, where moth and rust consume and where thieves break in and steal...For where your treasure is, there your heart will be also" (Matt 6:19, 21).

It is important for us to ask regularly: What moves my heart; where is my treasure? Caitlin's heart, moved by the need of others, cannot *not* see suffering and not respond to it. While her parents might insist that she continue in the school where she is learning so much about her tradition, neither they nor we can afford not to hear her prophetic call: a church that does not root itself in the "fundamental option for the poor" is not church at all.

Prayer

God of Justice,
Give me your compassionate goodness, your wholehearted love,
the tender conscience of a Caitlin and let me feel the injustice in
my world. Like the farmer and the sound of a cricket on the busy
streets of my life, let my heart hear what moves it. Remind me that
justice is not something we have already achieved but something
we must continuously strive for. Like Caitlin, let my quest for jus-
tice be enthusiastic, dynamic, impassioned, determined, and unre-
served. With the prophet Micah may I hear deeply your call to act
justly, love tenderly, and walk humbly with you, God of Justice.
Amen.

Doorway Reflections

• What does wholehearted love look like? How do we awaken that love in ourselves and others in our quest for justice?

- In what literature, history, and social teaching of the Church have you grounded yourself?
- Where are your treasure and your heart? What needs of others move your heart and demand a response?
- In what ways do you, personally and communally, express gratitude to God by working for the promotion of justice?
- How do you experience the church as rooted in the "fundamental option for the poor"?
- How do you act justly, love tenderly, and walk humbly with God?

A Back Door

Take my yoke upon you, and learn from me.
(Matt 11:29)

Tracy was barely sixteen and a brand-new driver when a car accident shattered her back and her life. A strong young woman, she was determined to gain as much independence as possible despite a spinal cord injury that left her virtually unable to walk.

A new student at our college, she worked in the department of student services, amazing all of us with her strength of will. When she told me she very much wanted to join us for the Sunday Eucharist, I assured her that we would help her in any way we could. While appreciative of my offer, she wanted only to know that the back door to the chapel was open on Sundays, giving her access to the elevator. That Sunday Tracy was in chapel before me, waiting patiently for Mass to begin.

The following Tuesday, Tracy's closest friend Melissa told me that Tracy probably couldn't come to church every Sunday.

It was just too difficult. To get to the 11:00 a.m. Mass, Tracy had to be out of bed by 6:00 a.m., to take a medication to activate her paralyzed intestines. Tracy did not want to bother me with this "minor" detail.

Tracy's story is a metaphor for me. Not only does her presence remind me to be grateful on a daily basis for the simple gifts of life, it challenges me to remember Jesus' gospel command, "Take my yoke upon you, and learn from me; for I am gentle and humble in heart...My yoke is easy, and my burden is light" (Matt 11:29–30). Yokes were used on beasts of burden in the ancient world. As long as they were carefully fitted, and polished smooth, they did not bind. Only when the animal fought the yoke did it choke.

The law was also seen as a yoke. Unfortunately, the most liberal of Jewish leaders in Jesus' day inflated the Ten Commandments into more than 620 laws that all had to obey to demonstrate faithfulness to God. Jesus made the good news simple. Love God and neighbor, he said, and you will fulfill the entire law and the prophets. Tracy tries every day to live these simple gospel challenges while living with a very painful yoke.

Loving God and neighbor takes dedication and determination every day as we give voice to the intentions of our heart. Tracy reminds us never to underestimate the power of Jesus and the human spirit as we listen inwardly to the truth that needs to be told of our own body and heart. There is a constancy in Tracy to "learn of Jesus," a willingness to greet life as it is and to be present to what is over and over again. Is this not the opening into the spiritual life? To be present, she cannot rush. Not wanting to disturb anyone and recognizing she must move at her own pace, she asks for a back door, a handicapped accessible entrance, to be left open.

In *The Talk That Rain Makes,* Thomas Merton notes that the "whole world runs by rhythms I don't know yet and I am going to listen for how long it rains." Tracy listens to her own body rhythms, patiently accepts the "yoke" of her own life, aware that even our "burdens" awaken us, teach us compassion, and transform us.

Prayer

God of All Yokes and Burdens,
Compassion expands our hearts and makes us aware that your yoke is easy and your burden light as we wait patiently with Tracy for a back door into your presence. Give us friends who gently open these doors. Do not rush us through them, and stay with us as we remain present to what is. Each day let us dedicate and give voice to our heart's intention to love you and our neighbor. We bow in reverence to what is. Amen.

Doorway Reflections

- Recall a shattering event in your own life. In what ways have you been confined? Who opens a back door for you?
- What simple gifts of life are you grateful for on a daily basis?
- What is your yoke? Are you aware of any harsh yokes you may place on others?
- For what do you wait patiently?
- Reflect on your day. When were you just present to what is?
- Who are the Tracys that open your heart? Pray for them.

 # Prison Doors

I was in prison and you visited me.
(Matt 25:36)

The clang, clang of heavy steel doors closing behind me was frightening and unnerving. Walking along a thoroughly antiseptic prison corridor, following a guard to a makeshift chaplain's office, I felt lost and was sweating even though the prison was cool. Though I had visited jails before, they were smaller county penitentiaries. This was Sing Sing, one of the most infamous prisons in the country.

Taking a deep breath, I realized that I was feeling more and more anxious and edgy. Would I be able to summon a guard quickly if the claustrophobia I was feeling became too much? What would I say to this man I had never met? Jimmy's mother stopped me after Sunday Mass and asked me to visit her son, assuring me that he was anxious to see a priest. Though I did not know Jimmy, I did know that he had been convicted of armed robbery, and that this was not his first time in jail.

As the last of the mountain-like doors banged shut behind me, I began to hear Matthew 25 in a very different way: "When I was in prison, you visited me." No comment on whether the visitor knew the prisoner. No indication whether it was a small or large place. Just "visit the imprisoned" if you want to live forever at God's right hand. As the guard stepped back to let me in the chaplain's room, a smiling man extended his hand in greeting.

Jimmy was small and wiry. Though obviously glad to see me, he too was anxious. "Welcome to Sing Sing," he said. "Ever been here before?" "No," I said. "This is my first time." "You never get used to it," he said. "It stinks, but I'm glad you came.

I'm worried about my mother. She's a very good woman but really ashamed to tell any of her friends that I'm here. I thought you might be able to help her."

I was stunned. I had been half expecting an explanation of his innocence or a request for money. Yet Jimmy wanted to talk, not about himself, but about his mother. What a different kind of doorway this was! My own anxiety had gotten in the way of my imagining Jimmy as anything but a criminal, a loser, who wanted to manipulate me. Meeting a man concerned about his mother and the shame he had brought upon her was a very different experience. Embarrassed by my own stereotypical thinking, I looked at Jimmy, not as a prisoner but as another image of the Risen One. Could this have been why Jesus wanted us to visit the imprisoned? Did he know that ministers always seem to get more from their giving than they themselves give and even occasionally met Christ himself?

Because they knew him as a boy, the people of Nazareth thought they knew who Jesus was. "Is not this the carpenter's son? Is not his mother called Mary? And are not his brothers James and Joseph and Simon and Judas?…Where then did this man get all this?" (Matt 13:55–56).

People, even prisoners, change and grow. When we fail to recognize the goodness in others, it is not they who are cheated. We rob ourselves of finding Christ everywhere. Despite his violent crime, Jimmy was concerned for others, especially his mother. We would be wrong not to imitate him.

Prayer

God of the Poor,
I care about those in prison, but do I know them? And yet, I hear
your voice: "You feed me…you visit me…you welcome me." Let

my acts of charity not be distant ones. To follow you, God of the Poor, let me encounter the poor, meet them, be converted by them. Tutor my heart to empathize with those on the outside of my heart's boundaries. Expand my heart to be a place of homecoming for the stranger and to be more at home in strange places, even prisons. Amen.

Doorway Reflections

- When have you been embarrassed by your own stereotypical thinking?
- From whom have you received more than you gave? Who are the imprisoned in your life—physically, emotionally, spiritually? Yourself? Others?
- In following the God of the Poor, how do you encounter the poor, not in distant sentiments of charity but in concrete actions?

 # Doorways of Challenge

Be wise as serpents and innocent as doves.
(Matt 10:16)

Arnold was nearing seventy when his eyesight began to fail. A feisty fellow who fought fiercely for his independence even as his body weakened, he was also a very caring husband and father. Although his children knew that it was becoming difficult, even dangerous, for him to drive, none of them wanted the task of speaking with him about it. Arnold solved this dilemma for them.

One day he called his son Steve and asked him to accompany him to the doctor. Arnold had never done anything like this before. In fact, the doctor was a friend of Arnold's who, his children often thought, was working together with their father to deny the effects of Arnold's aging.

When Arnold and Steve entered the doctor's office very little happened. The doctor did a perfunctory examination, proclaimed Arnold as healthy as any seventy-year-old with a tendency to congestive heart failure, and told him to come back in two months. Throughout the visit Steve said nothing nor was he surprised by what he experienced. He and his dad drove home in silence. When they arrived, the entire family had gathered for a meal. After the prayer, Arnold looked every member of his family in the eye, smiling and nodding ever so slightly when he came to Steve, and then made a startling announcement. Insisting that the doctor would never be his friend again, he told his wife and children that the son-of-a-gun of a doctor had forbidden him to drive. While he was hurt and upset, he would accept the man's judgment.

Steve was deeply touched. Though the doctor had said nothing about driving, once again his father had found a way to protect his own dignity and his children's concerns. Knowing his sight was slipping but not wanting to admit it, Arnold simply blamed his doctor and thereby freed his children from further worry.

Mother Cabrini, a woman very much like Arnold, was renowned not only for crossing the Atlantic Ocean dozens of times, but for building hundreds of hospitals and establishing communities of religious women committed to the poor. She was also, as Jesus cautioned his disciples, "as wise as serpents and as innocent as doves" (Matt 10:16). On one occasion in Chicago, she bought a piece of land on which to build a hospital. Suspecting that city surveyors were less than honest in establishing the boundaries of the parcel of land she purchased so that they could use some for themselves or sell it to others, she invited reporters to accompany her to the place as she measured her property with a yardstick. It did not take long for city officials to announce that they had made a mistake in surveying the hospital property and would restore to Mother Cabrini and her sisters the proper boundaries.

While not all of us have the shrewdness of Arnold or the wisdom of Mother Cabrini, we can strive for more honesty in life. Children especially are drawn to adults who treat them with dignity and find a way to tell them about important life lessons in ways they can understand. Sometimes, in trying to find just the right words to speak to another, we either fail to communicate at all or speak in such a convoluted way that our message does little good. Remembering people like Arnold can help us accept Jesus' challenge not to worry about what we are to say (Matt 10:19) when we pray for the gift of honesty.

Prayer

Ever-Present God,
Even when seeing the growing disabilities in myself or another, I turn away. I deny them. For fear of hurting someone, I refuse to talk about them. Give me, Gracious God, the dignity and shrewdness of an Arnold to choose a different way in letting the truth be known. Awaken within me the sensitivity of a Steve to accompany others quietly as they face, accept, and share who and where they are in life. Challenge me to be simple as a dove in your presence. And for your ever-nearness, Ever-Present God, thank you. Amen.

Doorway Reflections

- Like Arnold's adult children, recall a situation where you avoided speaking for fear of hurting another. How was the situation resolved?
- Are you more like, Steve, Arnold, or the doctor in denying disabilities?
- How do you help others be free from worry?
- In what ways have you accepted the challenge of Jesus to be "wise as serpents and innocent as doves"?

Door of Mercy

By the tender mercy of our God, the dawn from on high will break upon us. (Luke 1:78)

Mark was born stubborn. Even as a baby he ate only when he was hungry even if it meant half a day between nursing meals. So it was no surprise one Sunday that he refused to join us for supper. Only three, he was completely committed to a project in our backyard sandbox. No amount of prodding from his mother was going to change his mind. When his dad tried forcibly to bring him to the table his screaming resistance frightened the other children. Mark, even as a child, was typically American. He not only wanted his independence, he demanded it.

There is a word in Japanese, *amaeru*, which, loosely translated, means "tender mercy." It is often used by Japanese psychologists to describe the proper relationship therapists ought to have with their clients. *Amaeru* implies a mutuality between and among people. The therapist is not simply an outsider searching for the proper questions to help individuals discover keys to unlock their emotional history and life, but a person who accompanies suffering people with understanding and tenderness. In Japan, unlike in North America, the point of life is not full and total independence but the ability to accept and live in dependent harmony and tenderness with all creation. Mark needed someone to show *amaeru* to help him experience life not simply as a battle for his own "way," but as a journey we take together.

Don't the Jewish Scriptures suggest the same path? The eleventh chapter of Isaiah records a prophetic dream that all of creation will find a way to live well together:

> Then the wolf shall live with the lamb,
>   the leopard shall lie down with the kid,
> the calf and the lion and the fatling together,
>   and a little child shall lead them...
> The nursing child shall play over the hole of the asp,
>   and the weaned child shall put its hand on the adder's
>   den. (Isa 11:6, 8)

Clearly, Isaiah wants us to remember how devastating it is to ignore or deny our dependence on one another. In fact, if we fail to recognize our mutual interdependence, especially when we are under siege personally or communally, our world will become not a place where wolves live with lambs, but a battleground where all creation is at odds.

No wonder Luke has Zechariah shout out after the birth of John the Baptist,

> By the *tender mercy* of our God,
>   the dawn from on high will break upon us,

to give light to those who sit in darkness,…
to guide our feet into the way of peace. (Luke 1:78–79)

Peace and mercy are Jesus' great gifts to his suffering people. *Shalom* in Hebrew carries a meaning much deeper than the word *peace* in English. Be yourself, he challenges, be welcome in my home and no matter how great your sin, go to all nations and proclaim the gift of peace to everyone. Despite his disciples' inability to accompany him at the hour of his greatest need, he forgives them and after his resurrection continues to offer them the shalom of God. We have only to travel together, like sheep following a shepherd, to have God's peace and know God's joy. If we honor, respect, and show tender mercy to all that is, we will "inherit the kingdom of God," and discover new ways to help the Marks in all our families join us at the table of the Lord.

Prayer

God,
Visit me and wrap your cloak of tender mercy around my shoulders as we whisper our love to each other. Help me invite all of creation under your protective garment and experience that we are one community, dependent upon you for life, dependent on others in living your life. Accompany and teach me to accept and live in interdependent harmony with all of creation. Rid me of my stubborn striving for independence. Shower amaeru, *tender mercy, on me. Amen.*

Doorway Reflections

- When and to whom do you offer *amaeru* to others?
- Like Mark, consider ways you demand your independence.

- How do you accompany others in this interdependent journey of life? Who companions you with tender mercy?
- Ponder your relationship with creation: dependent, independent, interdependent? Which Scripture speaks to you about your relationship with creation?

A Singing Door

Jesus told them a parable about their need to pray always and not to lose heart.
(Luke 18:1)

Like so many third world people, Lucia, though only fifty years old, looks much older. Born in the favelas of Rio de Janeiro, Brazil, she is now a housekeeping specialist at a college where each day she moves quietly, almost silently, from building to building cleaning. Until noon. At 12:00 p.m. exactly, in place of lunch, she falls to her knees in the back of the chapel and begins her daily pilgrimage. From there she moves down a side aisle, into our Eucharistic chapel where she eventually reaches the tabernacle, singing all the while in Portuguese. Often, when I am early for the daily 12:30 p.m. Mass, I meet her. She smiles politely but never stops walking on her knees or singing. Her goal is too important to be delayed or interrupted by polite chatter.

One day, however, intrigued and moved by her faithfulness, I sat down and waited for her to finish her prayer. I wanted to know about her and why she prayed the way she did. In halting English she told me that because she could not read she sang her prayers from her knees, trusting that God would appreciate her efforts and help her family and nation. Besides, she said, because God is so beautiful, God must love beautiful songs. Her eyes, which never left mine, shone as she spoke her story. If I were God, I thought, I would listen very closely.

No matter what form it takes, prayer ought to be a regular part of our daily routine. While few of us would be comfortable walking on our knees, there is a dramatic power to Lucia's prayer and story that challenges us to find our own "prayer paths." Every place I've been, there is a hunger among people to learn about prayer and to find a form that works for them.

Gaynell recently offered an all-day prayer workshop at a local retreat center that was oversubscribed. Conscious of their need to grow in faith and express their deepest needs and desires, women and men, from their twenties to their seventies, gathered to reflect, study, and pray together. In addition to coming from so many age groups, the workshop participants represented religious educators, justice and peace ministers, working women and men, and retired people trying to grow in faith and prayer.

The need for and desire to pray well is everywhere. Jesus recognized this in his own life. Not only did he steal away to mountaintops and "out of the way" places to pray regularly, his disciples came to him asking for help with their own prayer life. Even though they had the psalms and a long tradition of household prayers, they wanted more. So do we.

Those to whom we minister, especially as teachers, need us as mentors in prayer and the ways of prayer. When we enter our classrooms with clearly defined prayer corners, knowing there will be time for prayer before and during each class, they learn how important prayer is to an integrated religious formation. When how we teach is grounded in our commitment to walk a daily "prayer path," we offer our students a great gift: not only do we teach about prayer, we pray.

Prayer

God of All Prayers,
There is a holy longing in us for you. Coming to prayer is like com-
ing home to that longing and discovering that you long for us, too.
With Lucia we say, "God, you are so beautiful. You must love
beautiful songs." "Sing a new song," the psalmist says, and "come
before God." We sing of our deepest needs and desires, God of all
Songs. Help us to discover that prayer is your work in us and
through us for others. In you we stand, sit, kneel, walk, and beg
that you let your song be sung in us. Amen.

Doorway Reflections

- What is your daily prayer pilgrimage?
- Do you ever sing your prayer?
- Consider writing/praying a prayer like Lucia's for your family and nation.
- Take a moment as you imagine God paying attention to you. Hear the words God speaks.
- Choose one action from your daily routine. Then, throughout the day, pause before this activity and take three mindful breaths, becoming deeply aware of God's presence with you.
- Talk with a friend about where you are on your prayer path.

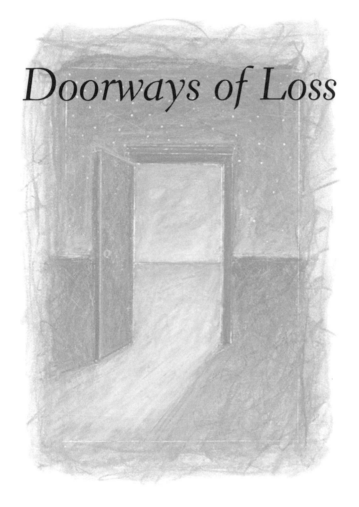

Doorways of Loss

Massaging hearts of tired spirits,
Patching lives torn by neglect...
(Like Jesus)

L oss comes to everyone. From losing the innocence of childhood to the sickness and death of family and friends, life and God challenge us to let go. Life is not something we can control or easily manipulate. Though we know this, we seem unable not to try to play God in order to avoid the pain of loss. While all of us seem able to help others by assuring them that they will survive their losses, we often do not know how to help ourselves. Good advice givers, we are rarely able to accept our own counsel.

In this section, *Doorways of Loss,* you will meet people who have faced loss: they have cried, groaned, even spit angrily into the wind of fate, but eventually they moved through and beyond their loss with the help of God, friends, and a community of faith. While not heroes, heroines, or icons in the usual sense, they nevertheless remind us of our own life tasks. We are to find God at the center of every darkness and proclaim God's goodness despite the helplessness we often experience. Listen to these stories, remember your own, and ask God for the strength to begin again.

A Grieving Place

The LORD is a stronghold for the oppressed,
a stronghold in times of trouble. (Ps 9:9)

Geri was hiding in the small foyer between the living room and the front stairs of her grandma's house. Surrounded by three doors, she could both close herself in when she was sad or troubled and have an easy escape route if people came too close. Every time I saw her there I was reminded of my own childhood search for a grieving place and I knew not to disturb her. Eventually, either from boredom, relief, fear, or genuine hope, she would rejoin her friends and family and make believe nothing had happened.

Most of us have grieving, pondering, reflective places in our lives. A garden that needs weeding or an attic that needs straightening can be a great solace to us when we are momentarily lost along the way. Grieving places give us the time and space to regroup, catch our breath, and repair our bruised spirits. They also assure us that grieving is a natural part of life that it does not pay to resist. Moreover, since each hurt is unique, we need to respect our own healing rhythms. Grief is brief or prolonged depending upon the nature of the hurt and our own personality. How we have dealt with other hurts, the number of losses that occur at one time, and quality of our support system also contribute to the pace of our healing.

Watching Geri searching for a way to repair her life, I began to wonder if Jesus had a "grieving place" as a boy and young man. Was Jesus really talking with the elders and rabbis the entire time his parents were searching for him, or had some new realization or hurt caused him to stay behind in Jerusalem? When the

Scriptures tell us that he went into the desert or on a mountaintop to pray, was he searching for some hard-to-determine meaning in his life? And when he asked his disciples to spend an hour with him in prayer the night before he died, was he grieving his failure to convert the leaders of the Jewish community to nonviolence and a different understanding of what prophets are like?

Mildred Tengbom in *Grief for a Season* speaks of a hospital bed as a grieving place. Because, in her wisdom, a little girl dying of leukemia knew that grief was natural sorrow that we need to let out, she asked a nurse for a crying doll. The puzzled nurse asked why she wanted a doll that could cry. The child told her: "Because I think Mommy and I need to cry. Mommy won't cry in front of me, and I can't cry if Mommy doesn't. If we had a crying doll, all three of us could cry together."

Because grieving is such a natural part of life, we all need grieving places. Life and faith are a series of transitions, each demanding a letting go before we can move on to and enjoy our next adventure. Take a moment to enjoy all the richness of your life and be especially grateful for those quiet places and friends who have allowed each of us the freedom to cry, mourn, and grow.

The word *comfort* means "to come alongside with strength." God comes alongside us and gives us strength in our grieving places, holding us, sometimes weeping, and always assuring us that joy will come again.

Prayer

God of All Comfort,
I search for a grieving place, a refuge of safety, a quiet, undisturbed place where I can pause and catch my breath. Suddenly, and all at once, with so many disappointments, failures, losses, I

need to be still and alone with you. Spread a comforter of love around me in this sacred place. Comforter of All, warm and repair my bruised spirit. Amen.

Doorway Reflections

- What do you have to grieve today? Where is your grieving place? What does this place offer you?
- Reflect on your own healing rhythm. Who supports your healing pace? Spend a moment in gratitude for all those who walk with you in grief.
- How do you bring comfort to others?
- Are you feeling bruised right now? Where will you go to catch your breath?
- Have you ever thought about Jesus grieving? Can you invite him to grieve with you?

Glass Doors

We have this treasure in clay jars.
(2 Cor 4:7)

Emily felt unbearably vulnerable. A family person, full of faith and deeply committed to her parish, she expected to be married forever. While she knew life was not always smooth with her husband Geoff, when he suggested they needed a trial separation, Emily was astonished. What had happened to them? How would she continue to make her children feel safe and loved? And to her surprise and embarrassment, she wondered what her friends and fellow teachers in the parish religious education program would think of her.

One morning, while trying to pray, a challenging image emerged: Emily saw herself living in a home with huge glass doors. Everyone could see her hurt, confusion, and heartache. Mortified, she wanted to run from her own imagination, change the doors, put up curtains, anything to hide from the shame she felt.

Vulnerability can be a terrible burden or a powerful opportunity. Sometimes it is both. So many of us depend, not on our own integrity and sense of self for our identity, but on what we do and how we appear to others. Emily deeply valued the admiration other women had for her abilities as a mother and teacher. While she was sometimes embarrassed to accept praise, afterward she was always grateful to God for the gifts she had received. Now, with all of this in jeopardy, she was very anxious.

Perhaps Jesus, returning home to Nazareth after preaching and performing miraculous signs all around Galilee, wondered, like Emily, about his new role, his new identity. Matthew writes that his neighbors "took offense at him" and asked, "Is not this the carpenter's son?...Where then did this man get all this?" (Matt 13:57, 55). What must the Lord have thought? How did he manage the rejection? More important, was he tempted to hide, explain himself at length, or escape the staring eyes and harsh judgments of his town folk?

James Fowler suggests that spiritual understanding ripens following the experience of what he calls "the sacrament of defeat." When everything crumbles, even a marriage we expected to last forever, we must acknowledge and accept that there are no ready answers to life's paradoxes, no way to escape suffering. But, Fowler suggests, if we allow faith to help us negotiate the ensuing dark night, a deeper spiritual energy can emerge.

Jesus does not want his disciples to defend themselves with their success, power, or money. Rather, he encourages them to continue to preach conversion and change. Emily, and all of us, need to hear the same message when it feels as if we are living in glass houses. Our identity in faith is not dependent on our success in marriage or career, but on our relationship with the Resurrected One and with the entire faith community.

It takes great courage and faith to live behind glass doors with the world watching but not really seeing us. Nevertheless, when we accept God's help, we discover that there are many people who understand, who have walked in broken places, and whose empathetic presence reminds us we are not alone. Like Paul with the Corinthians, we know that though there may be difficulties on all sides, and we see no answer to our problems, as "earthen jars" we carry the life of Jesus in us, and he is enough.

Indeed, all of us live in homes with glass doors. A parent drinks too much, a sibling is in a third or fourth marriage, a spouse is out of work for months, even years. At times like this, we struggle mightily with who we are and even seek to blame others for our troubles. But though it is difficult to accept personal responsibility for how we feel and how our life appears to others, it is the only authentic faith choice we have. God does not promise to free us from our vulnerabilities, but does assure us that we are never alone, that he will always be with us and will be our light in darkness.

Prayer

God of Glass Doors,
You see so clearly into my heart, through all my defenses and pretenses, and hear my pain of embarrassment. All-Seeing and All-Hearing One, you feel my rejection, my hurt and confusion. I am

so vulnerable, with pieces of myself scattered about for all the world to see. Give me courage to live behind glass doors, waiting for those with compassionate hearts who, if I let them, will be there for me. I am your earthen jar and I carry your life inside. Amen.

Doorway Reflections

- On what does your self-worth depend?
- When have you reached out to someone like Emily? In what situation have you found yourself like her?
- How do you manage rejection?
- How do you speak of the sadness that comes from impermanence?
- Do you find vulnerability a burden or an opportunity?

 # The Front Door

Strive to enter through the narrow door.
(Luke 13:24)

Almost swallowed up by his backpack, dressed in new school clothes from head to toe, five-year-old Jason walked proudly through his front door toward the waiting bus that would take him to school for the first time. Never turning back, he avoided seeing his parents, Jon and Lisa, crying as they waved goodbye, wondering whether their son was ready for this new experience.

Jason had wanted to go to school for more than two years. When his parents told him he would have to wait, he asked them over and over why he could not take the school bus with his older siblings. Unable to answer him satisfactorily, they simply promised that his time would soon come. Though unconvinced, Jason waited. Finally, the day had come. He was ready. His parents, though anxious for him to learn and grow with his friends, were not.

Going to school for the first time is a deeply important event in our society. As we walk through our front or back door, we signal that we are embarking on a new path, a new way of being in the world that will change us forever. While Jason may not be aware of this, his parents are. That is why they cry.

Not only are Jon and Lisa mourning the loss of their child, they are crying for themselves as well. No longer will they be the exclusive source of inspiration, education, and socialization in Jason's life. Jason and his new school friends will have the challenge of finding in one another a safe place and community in which to grow, change, and explore how to live in the world. While Jon and Lisa hope that school, clubs, and friends will help Jason weave his way through the tangles of life, they worry whether the values they worked so hard to develop at home will be strong enough to guide him when he is tempted.

Jesus had a word about all of this. Come in through the "narrow door" (Luke 13:24), he said. Stay close to your faith, your values, your God. Then, wherever you go, you will be accompanied by your authentic friends. Do not let yourself be misled by accomplishment, wealth, influence, or political power. Your strength lies in your faith relationships with one another.

While Jon and Lisa feel certain that Jason is entering school with these important gospel values, they are concerned with how he will sustain them in a much more diverse and complex world. Will Jason compare himself unfavorably to other children with more and better clothes, toys, and possessions?

While Jason will surely have moments of jealousy and envy, will the narrow gate continue to call him home to a family and faith community trying to live gospel values?

We often hear these kinds of questions while listening to small faith communities and every time we do they energize us with new hope. That people of faith continue to ask critical and reflective questions assures us that religious formation, worship, and service are helping believers struggle to live the gospel in their everyday lives.

Prayer

Weaver God,

I wave goodbye and cry. Am I ready for this new experience? Will this fresh path change me forever? Will it be the lens through which I see and love your created world? Help me weave my way through the tangles of life as I grow and explore how to live with you and love like you. Weave friends and relationships into my life to help me find and walk through the narrow door. Amen.

Doorway Reflections

- What is your narrow door: values, God, faith?
- What misleads you? What tests you?
- What authentic friends accompany you through the narrow door?
- Describe the door through which you walked on your own first day of school. Recall your own weepy sending of a child to school, moving from your parents' home, or a career change you made. How do life's passages fold and unfold in your everyday life?

Doors of Trust

Into your hand I commit my spirit,...
O LORD, faithful God. (Ps 31:5)

Saadia was devastated when her husband, Roger, only forty-one years old, was diagnosed with metastatic lung cancer. Though not religious, but wanting to accompany her husband spiritually along the terrifying journey ahead, she prayed hard that God would save her husband from what he called his "violent and unwelcome guest."

Her family, from whom she had separated many years ago, was of little help. Roger's family, on the other hand, was almost too helpful. Deeply pious, they flooded her with rosaries, novenas, and scapulars, and called her every time there was a healing service or Mass within a hundred miles. Saadia felt lost, a child in a mammoth mall where every store looked the same but none sold what she was looking for.

After six months of fruitless treatment, when it became apparent that Roger was going to die, Saadia sunk into a terrible depression. Though she functioned, getting their nine-year-old daughter Amy off to school and preparing simple meals, she felt nothing and sought the comfort of sleep whenever she could. Roger, meanwhile, became the caregiver for Saadia and Amy, cleaning up after every meal, doing the laundry, and refusing to talk about anything but how Saadia was feeling. When Roger finally died, less than a year from the time his cancer was diagnosed, Saadia was so broken that her relatives wondered whether she could even care for her daughter.

Then, at the funeral Mass, in a moment of stunning simplicity, Saadia began to heal. Amy, her hand wrapped tightly in an ace bandage after falling at school and spraining a finger, leaned her head on her mother's shoulder and looked to her for help. Saadia smiled, kissed Amy, and began to unwrap her daughter's hand. Watching this gentle action, it was as if Lazarus, wrapped in his burial clothes, was emerging from the tomb. Saadia and Amy smiled at each other, their bond renewed, and held each other's hands.

At the end of Mass, though she told her friends she could not possibly do a eulogy, Saadia approached the podium and began to speak. Thanking everyone for coming, and thanking God for Roger's goodness, she told us in a soft but very strong voice that she, Amy, and God would find a way to heal each other. When Saadia sat down, we all knew that we had witnessed a powerful moment of grace and transformation.

The Gospels are full of such pictures. Besides Lazarus, we meet the woman whose only son is being buried (Luke 7:12–16), the blind man by the side of the road (Mark 10:46–49), the newly married couple at Cana (John 2:1–10), the woman who touches the hem of Jesus' robe (Mark 5:26–28), and so many others. Death and illness, while undeniably terrifying and dark, can sometimes be the only way people are cleansed of their fears and tendency toward self-absorption. Until we reach that moment in life when we not only want but need God at the center of our consciousness, we can never experience the fullness of grace and the God whose love is total, unconditional, and gratuitous.

One wonders what happened to the people in the Gospels after Jesus' intervention. Did they return like Saadia and the one leper out of ten who was cured to thank the Lord? Will we?

Prayer

Trusting God,
Devastated. Terrified. Lost. Depressed. Feeling nothing. Like
Saadia, I, too, seek the comfort of sleep when my world begins to
crumble through illness and death. I am startled by my weakness.
What are you saying to me, God? What do you want me to see? to
accept? How do you want me to grow and love more? Let me hear
your voice: "You are not alone. I am with you as you discover more
about yourself." Give me compassion for myself, for Saadia, for
others who suffer. Bathe me in your total, unconditional, gratu-
itous love. "Into your hand I commit my spirit,…O LORD, faithful
God." Amen.

Doorway Reflections

- In what life situation have you felt like a lost child in a mammoth mall? Whose hand held yours and helped unwrap your
hurt/grief/depression?
- How have you given witness to a moment of grace in your life?
With which gospel story do you identify right now?
- How have you experienced the simplicity of God's intervention in your life?
- Speak of a time when you wanted and needed God's love at
the center of your consciousness and being.

The Aching Place

You will do well to be attentive to this as to a lamp shining in a dark place, until the day dawns and the morning star rises in your hearts. (2 Pet 1:19)

Lara was almost eighty but still spry and able to care for herself. Widowed at seventy-two, she missed her husband Ed badly and thought of him every day. Though his absence felt like a large hole inside her heart, after eight years she was slowly learning to treasure it.

Lara often wondered what expert had written that unless grieving was over in about a year the survivor should seek in-depth counseling.

When her granddaughter Emma found Lara crying one day and asked if she was okay, Lara told her she was fine, that tears were natural and good and she hoped people would cry for her when she died.

"Are you going to die, Grandma?" Emma asked.

"Not right away, Emma, but someday, yes, and I'll be glad to see Grandpa Ed and the both of us will pray for you and your family."

Lara had always been committed to honesty and hoped her daughter Jean would not be angry with her frankness with Emma but she knew no other way. Though death was painful, it was also natural, ordinary, and necessary.

Despite her aching, Lara was a joyful woman. In prayer she often identified with Mary's delight at the birth of Jesus and wondered whether Mary was as fascinated by Jesus as she was by her children and grandchildren. Only prayer, she thought, got her through the difficult times in her life and only prayer sustained her now.

How fortunate Emma is to have such a wise and honest grandmother in her life. In its own way grieving was a gift challenging her to let go and love again. With Lara we might ask: "What does this pain have to teach me?" William Worden in *Grief Counseling and Grief Therapy* suggests there are four tasks in mourning:

- to accept the reality of loss
- to experience the pain of grief
- to adjust to an environment without the lost person
- to reinvest emotional energy in life

Lara is learning to reinvest and find joy, gratitude, and a new appreciation for life.

Aging is not a disease. Neither is grieving. We do not have to treat them with emotional or spiritual antibiotics or surgery. Aging and grieving, when seen through the eyes of faith, can be gifts from God reminding us of our neediness and challenging us to pay more attention to God at work, prayer, and play.

Death's naturalness and necessity is one of the fundamental truths of life and our faith. Speaking about his own death and ours, Jesus says, "Unless a grain of wheat falls into the earth and dies, it remains just a single grain; but if it dies, it bears much fruit" (John 12:24). The Hindu poet Tagore reminds us: "Death is not extinguishing the light. It is putting out the lamp because the dawn has come." If we learn to call upon our loved ones in the communion of saints, the sooner will we become aware of the first streaks of dawn and take notice of the morning star rising in our hearts.

Prayer

God of Aching Places,
Can aging and grieving be gifts from you, God? Sometimes I say
yes, but often I run away from my aching heart. Let me know that
painful experiences are not diseases but simply a part of the ordi-
nary and natural processes of life. Give me the honesty and
courage to speak of my losses and diminishments. Let dawn come
and let your morning star rise gently in my hurting heart. I lack for
nothing in you, God of All Aches. Amen.

Doorway Reflections

- In what way have you learned to treasure the aching places of
  your life? How has pain been a teacher for you?
- What is your reaction to your parents' or your own aging
  process?
- What is your awareness of the communion of saints, especially
  those who have died, praying for and loving us today?
- What or who helps you in your aching times?
- How you do experience and explain death as natural and ordinary?
- Like Lara after loss, where have you found a new appreciation
  for life and felt the morning star rising in your heart?

The Old and New Door

See, I am making all things new. (Rev 21:5)

The door on her family's old summer cottage was hanging
askew. Jen had come here just to look and remember. She
thought it would help her let go of Patty, her youngest daughter,

who had left for college the previous weekend. But now she wanted to walk around inside again.

Not able to either close or open the door, Jen first tried lifting it, then pushing it; finally, she kicked it. Nothing worked. Frustrated by her weakness, Jen breathed in, made herself as thin as possible, and slipped into a once precious space and never-to-be-forgotten memories. Walking around the empty front room, she remembered every detail. Plastic teal furniture that stuck to you when you got up and poorly crafted watercolors of ocean sunsets on the walls. Jen loved the place and the time she had spent there with her family.

As she walked to the kitchen that overlooked the bay, she began to cry, letting out the loss of her youngest child. Jen had assured everyone that she was looking forward to a childless home and a kitchen that would be the same as she left it when she returned from work, but her spirit knew better. She was entering a time of important transition and she was afraid. How would she define herself? What would she and her husband Dan talk about? What would it be like to sing in the choir without hearing any of her children's voices around her? Would she get stuck like the old door, unable to move in or out?

Ancient peoples used small bottles to catch their tears when visiting suffering friends, enabling them to identify symbolically and tenderly with the sick as Jesus did. While some today identify tears with weakness, they can actually be a sign of strength as we try to express our compassion for others. Like Jen, we try not to be afraid to let our cleansing tears help us put our loss in a special place so that we can go on with our lives. Psalm 56:8 echoes these sentiments: "You have kept count of my tossings; put my tears in your bottle."

Though pained and tearful, Jen will have to learn that God knows and loves us in all our sadness and fear, and opens to us when we are most in need. The same will be true for all of us if we allow God to show us where we are stuck and how we can let go.

Prayer

God of Old and New,
Sometimes, like an old door in need of mending, I hang askew—
stuck, unable to move. I am afraid in this vulnerable, in-between,
threshold space and time and I cry out my loss. Your spirit chal-
lenges me both to cherish the memories and to let go, trusting you
will open a new window. I sit and wait. Healing Spirit, hurry and
mend me. Amen.

Doorway Reflections

- When have you breathed in, made yourself thin, and slipped into a precious space of never-to-be-forgotten memories?
- What loss have you let out through tears? When have you offered your bottle of tears to another?
- What stuck door are you unable to open or close? What window could be opening for you?

Doors of Acceptance

For we walk by faith, not by sight.
(2 Cor 5:7)

Pete's stroke was devastating to his family. Closely knit, compet-itive, and fiercely loyal, they were determined to nurse their father back to health. Setting up schedules for each of the six children to be with him at least ten hours a day, they were convinced that if they stimulated their father with conversation about matters he had always found interesting, they would enable him to recover and live a productive life.

Nothing worked. Not only did their dad not recover quickly, he deteriorated. He had four or five serious infections and no matter how hard he tried, he could not swallow even a few ounces of water. His wife, Evelyn, overwhelmed by the sickness of the man she had built her life around and frustrated that no amount of pushing and prodding seemed to help, sank into a deep depression.

One afternoon, while her youngest daughter Jenny was visiting, Evelyn began to talk about her frustrations, anger, and loss. Jenny listened quietly for a long time. Finally, Evelyn paused. Jenny took her mother's hand and said, "Mom, Dad is not going to get much better than he is right now. I know he wants to try but he gets tired so easily and falls asleep in the middle of his therapy. I think we need to accept where he is right now and enjoy what little he is able to do."

"How can you say that, Jenny?" Evelyn asked. "We have to keep trying."

"I didn't say we should stop trying," Jenny responded, "only that we need to accept Dad for who he is now, not what he used to be or what we want him to be."

Evelyn began to cry and then to sob. Jenny held her mother for a long time. "I know you're right, Jen, but it is so hard to accept. I feel like I'm giving up on Dad and he never gave up on us." Turning to Pete, Evelyn saw that he was crying, too. Through his tears, he whispered. "It's okay I'm okay I love you," then closed his eyes.

Illness to family members can be a terrible burden. Our faith tradition, while acknowledging the difficulty of suffering, suggests a different response. The Scriptures challenge us to remember that "we walk by faith, not by sight" (2 Cor 5:7), and that Christians must "take up their cross" (Matt 16:24) and follow Christ.

The poet Rainer Maria Rilke echoes this: "We need, in love, to practice only this: letting each other go. For holding on comes easily; we do not need to learn it." In fact, we seem instinctively to hold on, to try harder. Like the hero in *The Little Engine That Could*, we try to overcome all obstacles, unable to discern what is helpful and what gets in the way.

Yielding and letting go is the only way we learn to trust. It is not something we do but part of larger process of life, the time work of the Spirit in us. There is

> a time to embrace, and a time to refrain from embracing;
> a time to seek and a time to lose;
> a time to keep, and a time to throw away. (Eccl 3:5–7).

When we breathe in—grateful for life in whatever form—and breathe out—yielding our cares to God, to the people whose concerns we carry in our heart, we recognize the wisdom of Jenny's words. Letting go is not optional in this life, any more than exhalation is optional to breathing. Jenny unlatched a yielding door and drew her mother into a safe listening and crying place where she could learn to accept her husband's terrible ordeal.

Prayer

God of All Acceptance,
Things are not what they used to be, or what I want them to be.
My heart is heavy with the pain of loss and change. Holding on

comes so much more easily than letting go. Send me your Spirit in a Jenny who can provide a safe listening and crying place to help me accept what is. Strengthened by your love, let me breathe in, grateful for life in whatever form, and breathe out, letting go of my frustrations and cares and placing them into your hands. Amen.

Doorway Reflections

- What does your yielding door look like? Where does it lead?
- Who is the Jenny in your life?
- How do you discern time of being with or doing for?
- Tell your story of walking by faith not by sight.

 # The Anxious Door

Even though I walk through the darkest valley, I fear no evil; for you are with me; your rod and your staff—they comfort me. (Ps 23:4)

Tamisha had always been a gentle person. Committed to her family and church, she worshiped regularly, volunteered at the local food pantry, and was a member of her parish's youth council. The anxiety attacks that she first felt at a youth council meeting took her by surprise. Dizzy and a little disoriented, she excused herself, saying she didn't feel well. Sure that she would feel better when she got home, Tamisha was surprised by the second attack in her own bedroom. Unable to sleep, she felt closed in and jumpy. Only after hours of tossing and turning did she fall asleep from exhaustion.

Embarrassed by her newly developing "weakness," Tamisha said nothing to anyone. Though she got through the work day as a medical technician, she felt very uncomfortable at supper with her mother and sister. What is going on? she wondered. Afraid she was going crazy, she knew she would have to trust someone.

That night Tamisha opened her Bible to the passage where Jesus visits the home of Martha and Mary. Though she longed to sit at Jesus' feet like Mary, she identified more closely with Martha. Hearing Jesus say, "Martha, Martha, you are worried and distracted by many things; there is need of only one thing" (Luke 10:41–42), gave her the strength she needed to share her new fears with her best friend Sheba.

The next day, as she began to tell her story to Sheba, Tamisha felt the cloud begin to lift. Sheba assured her that she was not crazy, but did encourage her to seek counseling and promised to walk with her on this new path. In the ensuing weeks and months, what began as terror slowly changed into compassion for herself and those countless women and men who suffer from anxiety.

The great paleontologist Pierre Teilhard de Chardin, SJ, whose books acknowledge his own anxiety, advises: "Don't force on, as though you could be today what time will make you tomorrow. Give the Lord the benefit of believing that God's hand is leading you, and accept the anxiety of feeling yourself in suspense and incomplete."

Teilhard might also encourage us to take a prayer walk through anxiety with the comforting words of the psalms, which so often speak to the anxiety of the human heart. No need to have a walking stick, says the psalmist (23:1–4); the shepherd's rod and staff, and the shepherd himself, protect and support us in our walk through life's darkest valley. While walking and praying the psalms, put one foot in front of the other; take one mindful conscious breath after another; speak to God and let God speak to you or embrace you. One step, one breath, one word, one embrace, after another and another. Prayer walking is an exercise of the whole person that helps us walk through our most painful experiences and feelings.

Sometimes, when we find the strength not to run away, the most difficult moments of our lives become gifts of insight and paths of transformation. Jesus' own willingness to admit his fear and anxiety while enduring suffering and death in obedience to his Father is clear evidence of this. That must also be our prayer, a petition that Tamisha models powerfully.

Prayer

God of All Walks,
Tossing. Turning. I am weak and exhausted through this night of anxiety. I do not know where to turn. Help me to pray this night verse of John Henry Newman with all those struggling with anxiety:

> *Lead, kindly Light, amid the encircling gloom,*
> *Lead thou me on!*
> *The night is dark, and I am far from home—*
> *Lead thou me on!*
> *Keep Thou my feet; I do not ask to see*
> *The distant scene; one step enough for me.*
> *I was not ever thus, nor prayed that Thou*
> *Shouldst lead me on;*
> *I loved to choose and see my path; but now,*
> *Lead thou me on!*
> *Amen.*

Doorway Reflections

- In times of anxiety, how do you trust? To whom do you speak your fears?
- What new insight about yourself have you gained during anxious times?
- How does prayer walking speak to you?
- What brings you hope and comfort when you travel the "valley of darkness"?
- To whom have you offered a traveling stick?

Doorway of Paradox

Unless a grain of wheat falls into the earth and dies, it remains just a single grain; but if it dies, it bears much fruit. (John 12:24)

Although he grew up poor in the inner city, Enrique considered himself a man of privilege. Not only did he have access to adequate housing, education, and medical care, but both his parents had been actively involved in his life and challenged him to make a difference in the world. After graduating from college, committed to giving "from his substance," he joined the Peace Corps and chose to stay in Africa for several years after his Peace Corps days were over. Returning to the United States, he worked as a consultant to a firm that was actively involved in making clean water available to remote villages in Africa.

Then his world collapsed. The firm for which he worked changed ownership and direction and his skills were no longer needed. Confused and hurt, he began to look elsewhere for work, with little success. He even considered returning to Africa to work, but his wife and children had deep roots in their community and wanted no part of international travel or living. Enrique felt helpless. The New Year was coming and he had little to look forward to. That's when his youngest daughter, Sama, stepped up and helped him see life very differently.

Every year Enrique's wife, Althea, invited her family to participate in a New Year's ritual. In a large book, she would list all the struggles and sufferings of her family on one page and all its successes and triumphs on another. Each family member was also invited to add to the list. Without thinking, Althea put the loss of Enrique's job on the page marked "Struggle," but her daughter Sama thought otherwise. She moved the loss of her dad's job from the struggle page to the success page with a note that said "Let's talk."

That evening, after the family gathered to pray for the faith to let go of its sufferings and enter the New Year with hope, Sama spoke. Telling her family how much she often missed her dad when he traveled for months at a time, she said she was so happy to see him every night that she couldn't think of his job loss as a suffering but as a triumph. She liked having him around, found his presence comforting, and really enjoyed the family fun they could now have.

Enrique was near tears listening to Sama. Though still worried about what he would do to help provide for his family, he also knew that his biggest dreams had been fulfilled. Family had always been important to him. His parents insisted on family time and he and Althea did the same. That Sama had heard their insistence on doing things as a family not as a rigid call to be together all the time but as a way to enjoy one another's company was a great triumph indeed.

How often in all our lives what first appears as loss becomes real gain. In fact, this is one of the great themes of the Bible. Abraham has to leave his homeland in obedience to God, but is promised that his children will populate the earth. Only after Moses reluctantly challenges Pharaoh are the Jewish people set free from slavery in Egypt. And for Christians, Jesus says it over and over again: "Unless a grain of wheat falls to the ground and dies," it cannot bear fruit.

Prayer

God of Paradox,
Guide me, All-Seeing God, through all the collapses of my life.
Give me patience to wait for eyes to see and a heart to welcome
your movement in me from loss to hope. Struggle to triumph.
Appearances and first responses can be deceiving. Send me a
Sama in my life to wipe the dust from my eyes, and people to
bring me home again to the passion of living as family and com-
munity. I am humbled and filled with gratitude to be led again
into the depths of who and where you are in my life. Amen.

Doorway Reflections

- What are your rituals for transition times?
- Review your own struggles and successes. Like Sama, was there someone who helped you to see them differently?
- How do you let go of sufferings and continue to walk in hope?
- Where, how, and through whom are you experiencing God's guidance in your life right now?
- Reflect on the paradox of the single grain of wheat.

Doorways of Voiceless Gratitude

O give thanks to the LORD, call on his name, make known his deeds among the peoples. (1 Chron 16:8)

It happened again last week. Making the annual report at the Sunday Eucharist, the parish council president thanked the priests for doing such a good job, reminded the parish how lucky it was to have such dedicated and caring administrators, and forgot to mention the laypeople on staff. Susan's parish had five pastors come and go during her years as director of the RCIA, but she remained. Each time a new pastor arrived, she was patient, listened to his dreams and anxieties, and then was forgotten. Like an umpire in a baseball game, she did her job well but was rarely noticed or applauded. Like so many other laypeople in the church, she was faceless and largely voiceless.

Not the type to seek praise, Susan knew that many people appreciated her work, but this year, as she was marking twenty-five years of service, was different. While she would have been embarrassed by something as lavish as a party, a mention in the parish bulletin would have been nice. Upset with herself for being disappointed, she tried to put this latest hurt out of her mind. When she mentioned it to her husband, he smiled politely but said nothing. Because Dave had regularly encouraged her to speak up for herself, laypeople in general, and women especially, his smug smile felt like another rejection when she wanted only a ounce of recognition.

Unfortunately, Susan's situation is not uncommon in society and the Church. Not only are laypeople often unappreciated in the Church, women who work full-time in the United States are still earning only seventy-two cents on average to every dollar earned by men. And the average wage of women working professionally in the Church is even worse. While acknowledging this disparity, some Church leaders absolve themselves of this injustice by suggesting that the "vocation" of parish ministers justifies their low wages. Susan had absorbed all this for twenty-five years because she loved what she was doing and believed that her life of service was not only helping people draw closer to God, it was an example for young people to follow. But being ignored one more time was too much.

Remembering to say thank you to those who offer us gracious, often volunteer, service is a fundamentally important Christian duty. Most of us insist that our children learn the words *please* and *thank you* very early in life. And we are right to do so. By reminding our children not to take another's kindness for granted, we alert them to the wonder and awe of God's gratuitous and unending love for us. God, we learn and teach our children, cannot stop loving us. Because we are made in God's image, the gospel challenges us to live lives of loving service to all, even those who ignore us or who are unable to show gratitude or appreciation, and in those situations where we are faceless and voiceless.

Prayer

God of Please and Thank You,
Sometimes I feel voiceless, faceless, ignored, unappreciated, unrecognized, and barely noticed for the work I do. It hurts. God, is this how you feel when I take you for granted and ignore your presence in my ministry? If I do not know how to be open and work collaboratively with you, then how can I do the same in my ministry with others? Give me a voice, your voice, to speak of your loving pres-

ence in me. Give me courage to speak your words to those who ignore, take another's kindness for granted, or refuse to recognize that in ministry the journey is a "we." Let no one be forgotten. Give us hearts of appreciation and gratitude for the way you work in, through, and among each of us. Let us together be your people. Amen.

Doorway Reflections

- When do you feel voiceless?
- Identify and reflect on the role of the nameless and faceless people in Scripture.
- How can you acknowledge and recognize the Susans in your parish? Are you able to find your voice when someone has again been ignored?
- What is your vision of lay leadership and of your own vocation in parish ministry working collaboratively with pastors and staff?
- How do you give voice to God's life in you?

Doors of Weakness

Open doors before him — and the gates shall not be closed. (Isa 45:1)

Though seventy-two years old and a veteran lector, Jim often dreaded reading in public. No matter how hard he tried to center himself before proclaiming the Scriptures, his rate of speech would speed up and his mouth would get dry. Sometimes he even had to stop in the middle of a sentence to catch his breath.

Nevertheless, though embarrassed by his anxiety, he continues to read the Scriptures every Friday in his parish church.

Jim reminds us of dozens of lay ministers we know. Jane continues to teach despite her speech impediment. When she first volunteered to help with our religious education program, she was an aide. She would set up the classroom each week, arrange flowers on the prayer table, and jot down Scripture quotes and the theme of the lesson on the blackboard. After she had been doing this for four years, I asked her whether she would like to teach a class herself. Hesitating, she told me she thought her speech impediment would make it impossible for her to teach effectively. Though she was used to insensitive people snickering at her, she wondered whether she would be a distraction to the children. Because I knew that Jane was bright and very creative, I assured her that her gifts would make up for any hesitation in speech.

Jane has been teaching seventh-graders for six years now, and though she begins each year explaining her disability to her students, she realizes her revelation is primarily for herself. Children entering seventh-grade already know her from her reputation as a dynamic and exciting teacher. They even ask to be placed in her class.

When Navajo tribespeople weave blankets they purposely make a mistake to remind themselves that life is never perfect. All blankets have flaws, as do all people. When God's call goes out to Moses, Isaiah, and Jeremiah, they all respond with fear. Moses claims to have a speech impediment, Isaiah thinks his sin will get in the way of God's word, Jeremiah says he is too young to speak for God. When Jesus takes Peter up a high mountain to tell him more about himself, Peter is terrified. We hear God's response to fear in the first letter of John: "There is no fear in love, but perfect love casts out fear" (1 John 4:18). Paul also reminds his listeners that "God chose what is foolish in the world to shame the wise" (1 Cor 1:27).

Not only do our shortcomings make us humble, they also remind us never to forget the gospel call to compassion. Recognizing and accepting our faults and weaknesses is a firm ground upon which to build sensitivity to others. People who are deeply aware of their own struggles make wonderful lay ministers because they never forget how difficult simple tasks can be and, like Isaiah, they "open the doors" (Isa 45:1) for others.

Prayer

God of All Shortcomings,
Though I am often embarrassed and anxious because of my fail-
ings, God of all Weakness, you never reject me. How extraordi-
nary! Your presence gives me courage to stretch, learn, and grow.
Expand my heart with compassion so that I may be aware of and
sensitive to the shortcomings of others. In our weakness, O God,
you are our strength. Amen.

Doorway Reflections

- What is your shortcoming, your thread of weakness in your own Navajo blanket?
- How and to whom are you able to tell your ongoing story? In what way has your weakness been your strength?
- Where and how do you find the courage, like so many men and women of Scripture, to open doors for others, even in your weakness?

Automatic Doors

I am like those who have no help.
(Ps 88:4)

Armed with two small children and a shopping cart, Gloria knew her day had really gone sour when the automatic door to the supermarket was not working. A single mother, concerned even before she went into the store whether she had enough money for the milk, eggs, and cereal her family needed, she felt like screaming. Only the night before, her mother Rita was found wandering in her nightgown in the street. Because Gloria had no money to pay for a private facility the trip to the state psychiatric hospital was Rita's third. Gloria knew the scenario well. Her mother would languish in the state hospital until the drugs made it appear as if she could return home safely.

The malfunctioning automatic door, therefore, seemed like a metaphor for her life. Gloria started crying, more from frustration than sadness. Being a single mom was bad enough. Doors not working was too much. Though her children tried to hug and console her, Gloria knew what she had to do. Scooping up her the little ones, she left the shopping cart in front of the broken door and headed for church.

Gloria often found herself in the back of church in recent weeks. Sometimes, if she was alone, she would even try to yell at God. The director of religious education in her parish had encouraged her to express her angry, hurt, and painful feelings openly to God and, though slightly uncomfortable, Gloria opened her Bible and prayed Psalm 88 aloud. With her children beside her, she cried out:

> O LORD, God of my salvation,
>   when, at night, I cry out in your presence,
> let my prayer come before you;
>   incline your ear to my cry.
> For my soul is full of troubles,
>   and my life draws near to Sheol.
> I am counted among those who go down to the Pit;
>   I am like those who have no help. (vv. 1–4)

That was enough. Gloria's tears flowed again, this time with a measure of relief. She had often taught her students and children that when they were honest with God, God would help them. Now she experienced that same help. While her problems did not disappear, the overwhelming feeling of futility began to lift. Gloria breathed deeply the breath of God's healing strength and left the church, hopeful again that God would help her find a path of light.

Though most of us do not struggle with the kind of problems Gloria carries, all of us need to learn honesty at prayer, especially when struggles threaten to strangle us. Albert Camus reminds us that only "in the midst of winter" did he learn "that there was in me an invincible summer." And Helen Keller wrote: "Everything has its wonders, even darkness and silence, and I learn, whatever state I may be in, therein to be content."

Jesus practically begs us: "Come to me, all you that are weary and are carrying heavy burdens, and I will give you rest" (Matt 11:28). Still, despite the wisdom and counsel of so many who have gone before us, we insist on doing things our way. Gloria, one of the poor who, Jesus reminds us, will always be with us, not only goes to the Lord with her burdens, she teaches us to do the same. Listening to her story gives us the courage both to live life honestly and to pray our way through it.

Prayer

Summer and Winter God,
Sometimes I am so filled with troubles; they overflow. Where to
turn, what to do? I feel a scream deep inside but am afraid to give
it voice. How honest can I be with you, God, with these painful
feelings? I am confused but feel the tug of your call imploring: come
to me. Here are my burdens, my insistence on doing things my way.
Breathe your healing strength deeply in me. Send a summer hope
in the midst of winter. Give me rest. Amen.

Doorway Reflections

- Has something like a malfunctioning automatic door ever been a metaphor for your life?
- What feelings do you find difficult to express to God? Reflect on your honesty at prayer.
- Where have you been weak, without strength?
- Like Gloria's children, who hugs and offers you consolation?
- Where have you breathed deeply the breath of God's healing strength?
- How did you discover, like Camus, your invincible summer?
- What burdens do you take to God?

Doorways to Safety

At that place he came to a cave, and spent
the night there. (1 Kings 19:9)

Emilio hated his childhood bedroom. Though now an adult, he
remembered how the thin walls failed to keep out the noise of his

parents' loud and very long parties. He also recalled the fierce arguments that finally led to his mother's fleeing into what he now knows was a safe house. Nor could he forget the anxiety he experienced in wondering whether he and his brother, Jerome, would have to live alone with their dad, whose drinking had often led to violence. Should he call the police, his grandparents, one of his teachers? The paralysis of not knowing what to do was terrible.

Often, when Emilio heard adult friends talking about all the enjoyment they had growing up, and the special haven their bedrooms offered for hanging posters and hiding their treasured "stuff," he felt cheated. His childhood bedroom felt more like a prison cell than a place of fantasy and fun. Worse, at times he could not even imagine what his friends felt.

So filled with memories of confusion and fear, Emilio could make no sense of others' tales of talking with friends long into the night or sleeping until two in the afternoon. From the time he was seven or eight, while friends slept their Saturdays away, he worked at his uncle's grocery store, restacking shelves and pushing a broom. Ironically, working seemed much better to him than staying in his bedroom waiting for his father to wake up, raging after another night of drinking. How could he recover the joy of his childhood without returning to the image of a safe bedroom that he had never known?

The Jewish community into which Jesus was born rarely felt safe. Occupied and governed by the Roman government, Israel did not feel like the promised land. When Jesus began to preach, his followers hoped he was the promised Messiah, someone who would fulfill all their dreams of a free Israel where they could raise their children in peace.

Like Emilio, the Jewish people badly needed someone and someplace to help heal them of their abused and battered history. Gary Paul Nabhan in *The Geography of Childhood* says, "a small sheltered space provides a sense of security and answers the natural desire for a place to look at things carefully. In a safe hideaway one's special collections of things can be examined."

Elijah discovers a safe hideaway in a cave as he runs from an abusive situation. Looking to find God and healing in the loudness of thunder, fire, and earthquake, he finally recognizes God's presence in a gentle breeze (1 Kings 19). This tiny whisper gives Elijah the courage to reflect on his life and "things" again. Though hiding his face in his cloak, Elijah stands at the entrance of the cave and welcomes a new beginning.

The need to heal from the wounds of childhood is a large part of every person's life. Unless Emilio finds a way to return to his childhood bedroom and let go of it, he will never really be able to make his own bedroom and the bedrooms of his children safe places. Emilio—and there is a piece of Emilio in all of us—needs to learn how to sit with the memory of his pain before he can give direction to his present life. Learning to pray in bed with his wife in the quiet of early morning would be a great place to start. Perhaps he will have to ask his wife for help in ways he resists. Perhaps he can invite his children to join him. Whatever he chooses, he needs to replace the terror of his childhood with the hope of making today different.

Prayer

God of Tiny Whispers,
We run, afraid and alone in the loudness, frantic to find your safe
house of love. In a hideaway place, give healing. Bring salve to the
wounds of our abused and battered history. Be our gentle breeze.
Shelter us beyond our fears from death into life. Amen.

Doorway Reflections

- Describe your childhood bedroom. What are your memories there?
- Like Emilio, was there violence and fear in your childhood home?
- Did you leave home every chance you had in the hope you could escape from your family and yourself?
- What would you offer Emilio or yourself for healing? Where is your place of safety today?

Doorways of Gratitude

Doorway saints, you nurture us
By sharing your bread...and loving us
unconditionally.
(Like Jesus)

Gratitude can be an elusive virtue. Most of us remember to say "Thank you" when others give us gifts or go out of their way to help us. But gratitude ought to be a deeply ingrained attitude that we cultivate. Taking time each day, even several times a day, to thank God for life, breath, the earth, the skies, food, shelter, friends, and family changes us. Gratitude helps us see differently. Eventually, when it becomes a habit, it changes us. We think not first of ourselves and our needs but how fortunate we have been to live, love, and serve God and others.

The essays that follow, *Doorways of Gratitude*, speak mostly of people and situations that call forth gratitude, those faithful friends who stir up the Spirit's breath within and among us, not simply as a balm to heal our sometimes heavy hearts, but as oil that strengthens, renews, and lubricates our lives for the doing of faith and the proclamation of gratitude. We have been blessed by God each day, every day, no matter how difficult our lives can sometimes be. Praying for the habit and gift of gratitude will help us to appreciate and share this transforming gift with others.

Doorway of Wonder

I will tell of all your wonderful deeds,
I will be glad and exult in you. (Ps 9:1)

Peter, all of three years old, followed by his smiling dad, burst into his grandma's house and shouted, "Look what we found!" His two-year-old cousin, Luke, was all ears and hands, rushing toward Peter, anxious to touch and hold these new treasures. But Peter was firm and clear. "No, Luke, you'll hurt them." By this time, everyone present was paying attention and wanted to see what Peter had hidden in his pillow slip of a sack. As if on cue, Peter reached carefully into his bag and pulled out an insect larva, a small stone fossil, and an eagle feather. "Dad and I found them," Peter exclaimed, "and we're gonna put them on the table when we pray."

Peter's grandma could hardly contain herself. Fascinated by nature's gifts even as a little girl, she assured Peter that they would do just that but he also had to tell the story of his odyssey. "Well," Peter said, "me and Dad walked through the woods and just kept looking for stuff. Dad found the bug shell and rock and I found the feather. Aren't they great!" "Indeed," Grandma responded, trying to give the reluctant Peter a big kiss, "they are great and wonderful." Tim, Peter's dad, who had been quiet until that point, suggested that he and Peter tell the other children about each of their finds and Peter was happy to oblige. "Eagles lose their feathers a lot but they grow other ones so they can still fly. That's why we can keep this one." And Tim followed very gently: "Fossils, or stones with impressions of shells, leaves, and insects on them, are very common here near the Hudson River. They were formed thousands of years ago, even before Jesus was born." The children and adults listening were fascinated and so was Grandma. "And the insect larva shows us how life changes. In order to fly the insect has to leave behind the protection of its first home. Kind of like a baby has to leave her mother's womb in order to live with us. It's pretty scary."

How important it is to spend time discovering life together with our children! What a great gift we can be to them on walks through the woods, fishing a quiet stream, or sitting in a garden.

And how like Jesus we are when we do this. "A farmer went out to sow his seeds…Look at the lilies of the field…You are Peter and on this rock I will build my church" are just a few of the images and metaphors from nature that Jesus uses to help us hear and appreciate the good news. Our ability to pay attention to creation's mysteries and communicate them through story helps us not only to appreciate nature but to understand the gospel better.

Peter and his dad, the disciples and apostles, and all of us searching for good news not only have to walk through woods to find our treasures; we also need the light of faith to discover their hidden meanings. All of this takes time and nothing is more important for our children than the time we spend with them.

Prayer

God of Wonder,
Your gifts are so extravagant. You cannot keep the secret of your goodness from us. Your gifts are everywhere: boundless and abundant. Slow me down for long walks of wonder. Open my spirit to the enthusiasm and delight of the child and the urgency to share what my eyes and heart have seen—gifts like a small stone fossil, an eagle feather, an insect larva. Through an insect you show me the need to let go of the protection of the known and grow and fly into something new. Wonder God, you are all that is good and the goodness that everything has is you. Wow! Amen.

Doorway Reflections

- How do you pay attention to creation's mysteries? When do you feel compelled to tell their story?
- What treasures have you found in a walk through the woods? Reflect on their hidden meaning for you.
- What nature images or metaphors from Scripture have deepened your understanding of yourself and the gospel?
- What kind of light helps you to see more clearly?

 # A Blessing Doorway

God saw everything that he had made, and indeed, it was very good. (Gen 1:31)

Arriving at the remote retreat center a full day early, I intended to speak to no one. The semester of religious education had been exhausting. Interrupted by the terrorism of September 11, it never seemed to right itself. Teachers regularly excused themselves from their weekly assignments or were late, the children seemed especially anxious and loud, and I knew something had broken inside of me. I needed time for rest, silence, and reflection, apart from my everyday life.

Shortly after my arrival, I visited the bookstore, hoping to find something to help me reclaim my inner self. Music was playing gently in the background. Intrigued, I listened closely for a few moments only to be interrupted by a light tap. "Do you like the music?"

"Yes," I murmured, never making eye contact, hoping the intruder would go away.

"What do you think it's about?"

"Flying," I replied without hesitation.

"How did you know that?" she asked.

"My father was a pilot."

"So am I," my visitor answered. "Do you have a moment?"

"Yes," I said, reluctantly.

The airline pilot told me she always says a prayer for her crew, the passengers, and herself, before taking off. I must say I have never thought of a pilot ever praying for me before takeoff! She also told me that flying across our country, she often passes over the homes of people she knows and sends a blessing to them. Again, as planes fly overhead, I have never thought of a blessing being sent to me! Hesitating, she then told me that recently, flying over her own homestead, she sent a blessing to everyone there. Then, not knowing why, she asked them for a blessing. Two minutes later a message over her earphones insisted she make a 90 degree turn and land as soon as possible. On the ground she learned that she had been directly in the flight path of the hijacked plane that would crash in Pennsylvania.

After spending several days with other pilots and crew members, praying, talking, and listening, she was exhausted and had come to the retreat center to recover. Transfixed, my unwanted visitor's faith, prayer, and caring had moved and changed me. Thanking her for her goodness, I left the bookstore and wandered the retreat grounds for hours, grateful to be alive and newly hopeful about the future.

How many pilots, butchers, auto workers, doctors, and postal workers stop each day in prayer and offer blessings as they go about their daily chores? Surely, many more than I recognized or acknowledged. I needed to be more grateful. Thomas

Merton insists that we harbor a hidden wholeness. What if, as Creator God insists, we are already good, very, very good?

While chance encounters rarely produce the kind of results I experienced, taking time to be grateful each day for God's simple gifts of water, air, light, and fire is absolutely necessary if we hope to live authentic gospel lives. I had been obsessing about things I could not change or control, failing, as the gospel challenges, "to see the goodness that God has made" in all creation. Good people abound, if only we pause to listen to them. And it is the story of good people that children must hear if we want them to know a God of graciousness and compassion. Terrorism and war may always be with us, but so will pilots, parents, piano tuners, and children who struggle every day to live the gospel.

Prayer

God of All Blessings,

Blessed. Here, now, in this very moment. Created by you, God of Goodness, we are very, very good, blessed beyond our own imaginings. Awaken our eyes and ears to see and hear, our hearts to give and receive blessings. Let us bless strangers, like this airline pilot, people we notice on the street, in the market, on the bus, at stop lights: "May you be happy. May you be at peace." And let us receive your gracious blessings through others. Amen.

Doorway Reflections

- When have you been heavy with fatigue, worry, fear? Where and in whom did you find rest?
- Who helps you to notice the blessings in your life? What is your prayer of blessing for another?

- Pray the Canticle of Creation in Daniel 3:52–90 and journal on your own blessings for God.
- With Merton, where do you intuit your own hidden wholeness? How is this affirmed and confirmed?

A Thin Place

Remove the sandals from your feet, for the place on which you are standing is holy ground. (Exod 3:5)

Adam raised his hand quickly when I asked about rituals celebrated at home. "I place the baby Jesus in the crib on Christmas morning. I really like that." Presuming I understood his family ritual, I asked Adam whether his parents always let him do this part of the ritual. "Oh, no, Mrs. Cronin. My parents aren't there. They don't seem interested." Startled, I asked Adam, "So you do it by yourself?" "No, Mrs. Cronin. My four-year-old brother and I do it together. We really like it. It's the best part of Christmas."

While I always knew that children had wonderful imaginations and that the busyness of modern life had made it very difficult for families to celebrate together, Adam's ritual unnerved me. At first I was upset. Where were Adam's parents, I wondered? Why weren't they involved with what had clearly become an important Christmas ritual for their children?

Reminding myself not to judge until I understood the entire story, I shifted to Adam. What a remarkable child, I thought. Though only eight years old, he already understood ritual and was grounded in faith. What could we do, I wondered, to foster faith growth in this little boy? Once again I realized that

God works where God wants to work. While I am convinced that God works best around and through family gatherings that are then gathered up in our parishes, Adam was clearly an exception.

Jesus suggested the same thing. When his disciples wanted to send children away from him, thinking he was tired, he said, "Let the little children come to me, and do not stop them; for it is to such as these that the kingdom of heaven belongs" (Matt 19:14). While we usually interpret this passage as a rebuke to his disciples and a challenge to live like children, perhaps there was something else at work here. Maybe the Lord himself needed to be refreshed by the living faith of little ones.

Watch children play alone in a garden or on a playground. When no one is bothering them, their sense of wonder can be remarkable to those watching from a respectful distance. They speak to the rocks, whisper to plants, and are fascinated by insects and birds. They seem to have a natural reverence for creation and the God who made us all.

Like children, we need to remember that certain places are sacred. The Celtic tradition call them "thin places" where the gulf between God and us is narrowed and we experience God's hidden presence more clearly. "The place is never chosen," religious historian Mircea Eliade notes. "It is merely discovered and in some way or another reveals itself."

Moses was searching for a lost sheep, not God, when he encountered the burning bush. Recognizing that the place was holy, Moses removed his sandals, offering reverence to a place that he did not seek but that chose him. Likewise, Abraham, Isaac, and Jacob each dedicated an altar and celebrated a ritual to honor the holiness of the particular place where they experienced the unexpected presence of God.

Like these biblical figures, little Adam became a "place-sensitive person," alert to the potential thinness of every place. His simple faith and gesture challenge us to keep walking the path of discovery and ongoing conversion.

Prayer

God of Place,
We meet you in gardens, playgrounds, burning bushes, and cribs.
Give us the eyes and heart of a child to discover and encounter you
in these thin places. Make us "place-sensitive people." With all the
Adams of your world, let us discover the gesture of placing the
baby Jesus in a crib on Christmas morning as holy. Amen.

Doorway Reflections

- What are your rituals for entering a sacred place?
- Recall "thin places" of death, birth, discovery, despair, and beauty where you encountered the presence of God.
- How do you become a "place-sensitive person"?
- What are your rituals for dedicating and marking a place as holy?

A Shoeless Place

Take nothing for your journey, no staff, nor bag, nor bread, nor money. (Luke 9:3)

A few years ago, an International Students Club that I helped lead sponsored a world peace coffeehouse. About thirty-five of us gathered in one section of the college cafeteria to pray, sing, dance, and listen to students and faculty share stories, poems, and songs that spoke of peace and its absence with power and passion. It was a gentle evening that lifted all of us with hope.

Sonia, a young woman from the West Indies, touched me in a special way. Shy and a little frightened, she had no intention of sharing herself through word or song. Content to set up the microphone, light candles, and help get ready for the event, she intended to sit back and enjoy listening to others.

But God had another plan. Her close friend Amy, born in China and a leader of the international students, had class that evening and could not join us. Reluctant Sonia was deputized to read something in Amy's name from the poet Martin Espada. As Sonia approached the microphone to read a satirical poem about Nike sneakers assembled in the third world for pennies, but costing as much as $200 in the United States, she slipped off her own shoes, telling us she wanted to identify with exploited children everywhere, many of whom had no shoes. She knew them, she said, because she had been one of them. Her words touched me but her gesture moved me even more.

Sacred gestures, especially when they are celebrated simply and clearly, often act as transforming moments for us. A child's bouquet of dandelions, stuffed into an old jelly jar and set in the middle of the kitchen table as gift to her mother; Moses' encounter with the burning bush on Mount Zion; Jesus telling us to take nothing for the journey; and St. Francis taking off all his clothes to identify more closely with the poor remind us without words that God is active in our lives and everything about today is different.

Ironically, in setting up the room, Sonia provided for others what she needed herself, an environment that fostered an awareness of the sacred so she could do in bodily action what her heart already knew. Her ritual gesture gathered up her own long-ings and used the ordinary to give life to the transcendent.

"Rituals," as Bernard Cooke assures us, "interpret our life and our life interprets how Christ is among us." Rituals help us make connections. Removing her shoes allowed Sonia to invite us into mystery, fresh understanding, and a deepening commit-ment to justice and peace. Rituals always begin with our need to express through story, symbol, and action our deepest emotions and intuitions. We do not try to capture God in them, but they offer us a means of relating to God or responding to God who relates to us.

In Noah ben Shea's *Jacob the Baker*, a woman asks Jacob if it is hard to pray and whether he always prays in the same way. Jacob tells her that indeed it is "difficult to get out of my own way." Prayer for him brings together what was never apart and is "a path where there is none....Ritual is prayer's vehicle." Sonia's prayer allows her to get out of her own way by standing barefoot, united with the poor and all creation, proclaiming justice while inviting us to do the same.

Prayer

God of Journeys,
Stories, poems, songs, and dance. Lighted candles, shoes, clothes,
and a burning bush. Dandelions. An old jelly jar, a signed ban-
ner. We know you hear us, Listening God, as we speak of our deep-
est understandings. Let these gestures interpret our life and let our
life interpret how you, Faithful One, are with us as companion
and friend. Transform us through the gestures of your love and
make us one with you and all that you have made. Amen.

Doorway Reflections

- In what way can you identify with Sonia? For whom and for what would you take off your shoes?
- In what space do you ritualize?
- What are some of your deepest longings? How would you express them through gesture?
- Do you always pray in the same way? Consider the way you already use ritual as "prayer's vehicle."

# Theater Doors

Blessed are your eyes, because they see, and your ears, for they hear. (Matt 13:16)

Jekyll and Hyde was to be Sarah's first big play. Enamored with acting ever since watching her grandparents and mother direct a children's theater, she was anxious and excited to see adults perform for the first time. As we entered the small community theater, I could not stop myself from stealing glances at her. She noticed everything, from the curtain to the klieg lights to the people handing out programs. Nothing was too small to enjoy. As I watched her spirit fill with gladness, I remembered my own first theater experience and the countless plays in which I had acted. The theater had always been magic for me. That it was filling Sarah with the same kind of energy pleased me beyond words.

Finally, the lights were lowered and the play began. Though it was not the most finished of productions, the players obviously enjoyed what they were doing. They sang with passion and danced with delight. Sarah laughed, clapped enthusiastically, and finally began to cry. Only later did I discover that the spirit of a young boy with Down syndrome captured her attention more than anything else. Clearly, the small company of actors had decided to give access to those with disabilities, not only by building a ramp to enter the theater, but by including them in the production itself.

And this was no easy task. Though the young man with Down syndrome had obviously practiced diligently to learn his stage directions and movements, he was often a half step slower than the other players and would have to hurry to catch up. But what impressed Sarah most was the ability of the players not to try too hard to help, thereby bringing too much unneeded attention to the young man.

On the drive home after the play, Sarah could not stop talking. She was grateful to us, committed to bringing more theater to our small village, and anxious to tell all her friends about her new favorite actor. My husband Jim and I were too near tears to say very much. We simply let her talk and plan and enjoy. Her happiness was enough for all three of us.

When given a chance, young people often have the ability to remind us of life's great lessons. Every person has dignity. No one should be excluded from living his or her dreams. The arts have the ability to point everyone, without regard to mental, emotional, or physical strength, toward awe and wonder. And when our imaginations are set free, we have the ability to know truth, a truth that sets us free, in an experiential way.

The stories of Jesus often challenged his listeners, the first of whom were mostly poor persons, to use their imaginations creatively in order to understand God's plan. "Look at the birds of the air; they neither sow nor reap nor gather into barns, and yet your heavenly Father feeds them. Are not you not of more value than they?" (Matt 6:26). Simply looking carefully at creation, with all its beauty and flaws, enabled the disciples to take another step toward the awesome goodness of God. Surely Sarah's enthrallment with the theater and all its players teaches us the same lesson. "Blessed are your eyes, for they see, and your ears, for they hear" (Matt 13:16).

Prayer

Creator God,
We sing with passion, dance with delight, and clap enthusiastically, as we embrace and welcome all of life in your community theater of creation. Awaken our eyes and ears to see and hear as Sarah did. Call us, God of all the Arts, to include and not exclude. Give us the gift of imagination and stand with us as we try to live our dreams. Continue to offer us the same acceptance and dignity in our own disabilities as you did for this young boy through this theater group. We clap enthusiastically for your presence in your theater of creation. Amen.

Doorway Reflections

- What energizes you? For what do you laugh, clap enthusiastically, and even cry?
- Like the theater group, how does your community welcome, accept, offer dignity and access to those with disabilities?
- As family and community, whom do you include and exclude?
- How do you avoid bringing too much unneeded attention when helping others?
- Who and what points you toward awe and wonder?
- What is the truth that sets you free?

 # Doorways of God-with-Us

*So then you are no longer strangers and
aliens, but you are citizens with the saints
and also members of the household of God.*
(Eph 2:19)

I wasn't sure what to expect when I visited Kathleen in the hospital. A friend called telling me that Kathleen's elderly parents
were both unable to visit often or find a priest to anoint their
daughter and asked if I could find the time to visit and pray with
her. A woman of about forty, he said, Kathleen was dying of
unknown causes in a horror of a hospital where the homeless
often are dumped and forgotten.

Visiting, however, was hardly the right word for what I was
called to do. Alone, on oxygen and in a fetal position, Kathleen
lay in her bed struggling to breathe accompanied only by a photo
of her as a young girl inscribed "with love" to her father. Though
clean and tidy, the room felt barren, filled with the smell of anti-
septics. I prayed for a while, doing my best to think of her in
more vital times and wondering what story the photo was trying
to tell. Then I sat down.

Fifteen minutes later I still could not leave. This is life, I
thought, at its most primitive and intimate. Kathleen, almost
exactly as a newborn, was unable to speak or respond to my
words or prayers, but how different these dying lonely moments
were from the joyful hours after her birth. What had her life
been like, I wondered, and who was thinking of her now?

Almost instinctively, I stretched my hand to her, praying,
blessing, and asking God to bless me with her life. Ministry, I

remembered, when authentic, is always mutual. Slowly a peace filled me. Kathleen's vulnerability and helplessness were indeed blessing me and, without my asking, many of my friends and family were coming into the room.

Gloria came first, mourning her seventeen-year-old son's suicide. Then Karl arrived, a very successful businessman who still has not had a sober Thanksgiving or Christmas. Karl was followed by Katie, abused by an uncle at seven, now counseling other victims and survivors. Lastly, my parents, long dead, and my first mentor, Bill, newly dead, entered the room. Together we sat and prayed, honoring Kathleen with the kind of dignity the hospital had stripped from her. Indeed, we were, as Elizabeth Johnson reminds us, the communion of saints, gathered together in faith without the limitations of time or space.

Faith is simple. It declares without excuse or explanation that God is good and present to each and all of us. God is Emmanuel, a hovering, abiding presence who gives us life and accompanies us to the top of every mountain and bottom of every valley. God is not a magician fixing Humpty Dumpties who fall off walls, but a nomad who lives on the edge of every life and society, making room in her tent for all those who need a home. Wrapped in her arms, like Kathleen breathing her last or presidents and popes making decisions that change the world, we have nothing to fear.

Prayer

Abiding Presence,
You are God-with-us, presence of love among us. Amid the fragility
and brokenness of being human, you are at-home God. In power-
lessness and poverty, you live. In our helplessness and vulnerabil-
ity, you are there. You are love in the ruins.

I honor you-with-us in Kathleen and all those beyond our understanding. In people like them, Nomad God, you live and have your being on the edge of every life. From these edges, I whisper for help, protection, and strength for family and friends in your communion of people who have already walked this faith path (name your own). *Welcome me into the ongoing river of companions seeking you and let me experience your love here in the ruins. Amen.*

Doorway Reflections

- How and when do you recognize God-with-us?
- Have you ever stretched your hand, prayed, blessed, and asked God to be blessed with the life of another?
- How has the vulnerability and helplessness of another blessed you?
- Authentic ministry is always mutual. How is this true in your own life?
- Who sits with you from the communion of saints when you need support, protection, strength?
- Is there a special space where you meet God?

Doors of Thanks

O LORD my God, I will give thanks to you forever. (Ps 30:12)

As the number of our birthdays increases, we often experience a greater reluctance to celebrate them. Such was my situation this year. Age, I know, is creeping up on me. Though my spirit rarely feels older, my body will not lie. I walk and think a bit more slowly, not altogether unhappy developments, but unmistakable signs of aging. How delighted I was, then, to receive a birthday package in the mail from my eldest daughter and her family.

Opening their gift, I discovered a lovely sand candle, beautiful in itself but made even more special by the note attached to it.

> Grandma, every year we miss being with you on your birthday. This year we decided to make a beach candle. We each found a shell on the beach that reminded us of you and we said a little prayer for you as we held our shell. We then put our found shells together in a sand candle for you to light on your birthday and hear us as we sing happy birthday. We love you.

Looking at the candle for the longest time, I imagined Claire, Tim, Sarah, Maggie, and Peter searching the sands for my perfect shell. What about the shell made them think of me? I wondered. And would I ever be able to light this precious work of art?

Simple homemade gifts that invite us to celebrate our love for one another and God through ritual can be marvelous invitations to faith growth. Not only do they speak of who and what we are, they allow us to remember where we've been, whom we've known, and how much we are loved. More important, they allow children to participate fully in the process of saying thank you without spending money.

People who join twelve-step groups like Alcoholics Anonymous know well the power of gratitude. They encourage their members to develop an attitude of gratitude in all their affairs. Attitudes are stances or postures we take. They are ways we present ourselves to others and to God. While at times we can have an attitude of haughtiness or arrogance, faith demands that we have a Eucharistic attitude, that we become a community that stands before God with heads bowed in gratitude and reverence. Meister Eckhart, the great medieval mystic, reminds us that if the only prayer we ever prayed our entire life was "Thank you," that would be enough.

Jesus himself would have affirmed children, grandchildren, and all people who recognize the need to speak of and live the love they feel by showing signs of gratitude in their daily lives. In all four of the Gospels, each time he breaks bread either as a way of helping hungry people or feeding his disciples at the Last Supper, he pauses to give thanks to God. Listening to the gospel, it is not difficult to imagine Jesus singing Psalm 30 with his friends, family and disciples: may

> my soul...praise you and not be silent.
> O LORD, my God, I will thanks to you forever. (v. 12)

Neither is it difficult to recall story after gospel story of people like the blind beggar and the bleeding woman who stand in awe before the Lord because they have been healed, helped, or given new hope. How well it would be for us to do the same!

Prayer

Good and Generous God,
We are so grateful for all you are and all you give. Thank you.
Enfold us in the garment of your love. Make us aware of the won-
der of your care. Clothe us in gratitude as your people. From lov-
ing hands, give us shells, sand candles, and light. Gently remind
us that we are to be your body on earth and to build up the spirit

of all your people. Amen. (Stand before God, head bowed in gratitude.)

Doorway Reflections

- What signs of gratitude do you give and receive? Like Jesus, when do you "pause" and give thanks to God?
- For whom are you most grateful in your life today?
- Recall a gift you received that speaks of who you are.
- Who are the people who love you? How do you celebrate your love for them?

Stairways of Memory

That one is like a man building a house, who dug deeply and laid the foundation on a rock. (Luke 6:48)

Maria loved her grandfather. Kind, strong, and loving, he was an icon to her as a young girl. Grandpa could do anything. He even built his own home and hers. Together with her dad, Grandpa had worked for months laying a foundation, constructing the frame, and making the rooms that would house her and her siblings. To her utter amazement he had also built a lovely winding stone staircase leading up to her home.

Maria loved to watch her grandpa at work, especially when he was building the staircase. Picking up each stone, he would look at it carefully and put it in place. Bit by bit a beautiful stairway emerged. Grandpa never seemed to measure when he built the stairway. From time to time, he would step back from his work, look carefully at what he had done, and then choose another stone that seemed to fit seamlessly with the others.

As a girl Maria was sure Grandpa had magical powers, and she never tired telling her friends about his wonderful staircase. Many years later, after Maria had lived in several different states and countries with her soldier husband and children, she had a chance to return to that first home. A bit apprehensive about what she would find, she was startled when she finally arrived on her old street in front of her first home. A Taco Bell had taken its place. The only thing left was Grandpa's stone stairway, which now led to a parking lot.

In tears, Maria walked over to the stairway and sat down. Her grandfather's presence came rushing back to her. His goodness and kindness, his skill, and his smile filled her with happy memories. Most startling was the realization that her grandpa was her present age when he built the stairway. Maria wondered whether her life had impacted her children and friends like Grandpa's had changed hers. Maria had caught perseverance, honesty, integrity, and care about the smallest things from Grandpa.

Were her children catching the same values from her? Would her grandchildren remember her commitment to family values and justice for all, especially those our society often rejects as lazy or worthless? Grandpa's staircase stood as monument to him and his goodness. What, Maria wondered, had she built?

Jesus tells us clearly to "build our house on solid rock," to make sure that we have a firm foundation in faith for all that we do. He also reminds us that people will know who we are by the love and care we show to one another, especially our enemies. St. Francis often cautioned his first followers not to worry too much about how they appeared to others but to "preach always, sometimes using words." Our children, we can be sure, will catch faith from us, not so much by what we say but by how we live the good news in our daily lives. Maria didn't remember much of what her grandfather said to her when she was a child, but she could still feel his love radiating from those steps. As she sat on the stairwell he fashioned so long ago, she felt a new determination to live her faith a day at a time with the same resolve Grandpa had exhibited in building his magical staircase.

Prayer

God of Memories,
Fit me seamlessly into your life. Give me a foundation in your love. Build a lovely winding staircase into the home you have already made in me. Let me catch your compassion, God, and your goodness and kindness. Like St. Francis, help me to preach always, sometimes using words. Let me feel the warmth of your smile as you fill me with happy memories of people in my life who by their faithful presence loved, shaped, and formed me. For them, I am filled with gratitude. Thank you. Thank you. Amen.

Doorway Reflections

- Who has built a stairway to the home of the heart for you? Who has changed your life?
- Like Maria's grandfather, in what way do you hope your life will impact your children and friends? What values do you want your children and grandchildren to catch from you?
- Like this stairway, what monument could stand for you?

Doors of Love

How beautiful you are, my love, how very beautiful! (Song of Songs 4:1)

Frank and Melanie were married ten years when they decided that despite the cost and effort of leaving their three children for a weekend, they needed to get away by themselves to renew their marriage commitment. When Melanie suggested they return to the hotel where they had stayed the night they were married, Frank thought it was a great idea. Even as they talked about their little dream, they became excited. When Melanie suggested that because Frank had injured his back in a car accident, she would carry him over the threshold, they laughed until they cried.

Frank immediately got on the phone to check the hotel's availability. When the hotel told him they would be happy to welcome him and his wife and even had a special weekend rate for couples celebrating anniversaries, their excitement grew. That evening Melanie placed their wedding photo album in the middle of the dining room table. After dinner she invited their three children to sit with them as they pointed out photos of grandparents, aunts, uncles, and relatives the children never met. They even paused for a moment to pray for the few wedding guests who had already died.

That night Frank and Melanie were very quiet and tender with one another. Pausing in front of their bedroom door, Melanie said, "You know, Frank, just realizing that you want to go away with me again is almost as good as a vacation itself. Hearing you laugh so freely, seeing the excitement in your eyes, and remembering how hard we have tried to live marriage and raise our children is very rewarding. I really do love you." Frank took Melanie's hand, kissed her lightly, and said, "I love you, too, my friend."

From time to time, all of us become disoriented and fragmented, and need something to knit us together again, to renew our commitment to God and each other. Jubilee years mentioned in Scripture did just that. Bells rang. Trumpets sounded in the morning. Debts and enemies were forgiven and all were challenged to "speak tenderly" (Hos 2:14).

The poet Rilke also reminds us that healing comes when "a love relationship offers space and freedom for growth. Each partner is the means of releasing the other. And love consists in this, that two solitudes protect and touch and greet each other." Frank and Melanie knew they needed a jubilee time in their marriage. Planning a simple vacation and looking at their wedding album with their children helped release their memories and opened a love doorway that reminded them of their personal communion of saints, their family, friends, and all the people to whom they belonged in faith.

Think about your marriage bed and bedroom. Take a moment to be grateful for your lovemaking. Pray for your spouse, even if he or she is no longer with you. While bedrooms can have very painful memories, they can also be places to which we let our spirit drift and remember the tenderness and hope. Bedrooms are places of creativity and passion, conversation and dreams. Dream again about what God can do for you and us.

Prayer

God of All Hearts,
We walk through your doors of love to renew the covenant. We rejoice in good times and embrace suffering. Thank you for our bedrooms, those places of tenderness and hope, creativity and pas-

sion, conversation and dreams where we offer and renew commitments of love. Release, protect, and greet our love for you in each other. Together, let us say and hear, I love you, too, my friend. Amen.

Doorway Reflections

- How do you renew your commitments? What gestures help you celebrate anniversaries?
- Does the insight of Rilke that "a love relationship offers space and freedom for growth" for both parties in a marriage ring true in your heart? Recall those love relationships that have brought healing.
- What dream do you think God has for you?

Doors of Grace

O give thanks to the LORD, for he is good; for his steadfast love endures forever.
(1 Chron 16:34)

Ronnie drank too much even as a teenager, but like most young people he thought of himself as invincible. While he often had a headache in the morning, that was the price, he told everyone, of having fun. Bright and funny, he talked his way through most of his difficulties. Because he was likeable, almost everyone was willing to overlook his addiction.

At twenty-two Ronnie went to alcoholic rehab for the first time, but thirty days was hardly long enough to change his life and lifestyle. Less than a day after returning home, he was drinking again, assuring everyone that he was not an alcoholic. He could "hold his liquor" and "drink with the best of them." Besides, he bragged, though he often fell asleep on the job and spoke too loudly and inappropriately, he never missed a day of work.

Then the bottom fell out of Ronnie's life. Attempting to string a clothesline while drunk, he fell three stories from his apartment porch. When he woke in the hospital he was completely paralyzed below his chest. Unable to move his arms or legs, with the help of deeply caring therapists, he finally learned to manipulate his wheelchair with his breath. That was the beginning of his conversion. One of the first things he did was "blow" his way to the chapel and promise God that he would be grateful for each day. The following Sunday Ronnie came to Mass. When I asked if anyone wanted to pray for something special, Ronnie asked that we pray for those less fortunate than us. I was startled. This man was for real.

Afterward, as we sipped coffee, Ronnie assured me he had been given the grace to live and he was going to make the most of it. He could have died. He could have continued to drink. Instead, he was with us and he was sure he had a mission. He had enough to eat, good people to help him in and out of bed, and a wheelchair to get around the hospital to visit, and he could get to Mass and pray. While the gifts he received each day were different from what he expected, they were, nonetheless, gifts.

Ronnie's attitude made me wonder about my own approach to life's struggles. Was I grateful for everything life presented? Was I willing to accept life on its terms? Did I take a moment each day to be grateful for the morning's first conscious breaths, for the ability and freedom to get out of bed, make coffee, pray in my favorite chair? Ronnie's life demanded that I think about everything I take for granted.

Our children's spontaneous laughter, awe over simple things, and transparency often teach us the same lessons. So does Paul. "Be filled with the Spirit, as you sing psalms and hymns and spiritual songs among yourselves, singing and making melody to the Lord in your hearts, giving thanks to God the Father at all times and for everything in the name of our Lord Jesus Christ" (Eph 5:18–20). Ronnie lives Paul's exhortation to the Ephesians every day. So ought we.

Prayer

God of Grace and Gratitude,
For all things great and small, the ordinary and extraordinary,
thank you. Your presence surrounds us. Bring change as we invite
the Spirit to open our eyes to the abundance that is already ours.
With the Spirit's sustaining breath, help us to be grateful, like
Ronnie, for everything life presents. And let gratitude give way to
simplicity—the desire to clear out, pare down, and live more sim-
ply. At morning light, we take a moment to breathe in gratitude,
letting it expand our hearts. As we exhale, we send blessings to oth-
ers and say: "Ordinary day, let us know you for the treasure that
you are, for in you is God." We bow deeply in gratitude for the
grace in all of life. Amen.

Doorway Reflections

- What grace have you been given to live?
- What initiated a change in your lifestyle?
- How do you approach life's struggles? Consider a time you accepted life on its own terms.

- For what are you grateful? Make a gratitude list, a mental and spiritual inventory of all that you have.
- In what ways do you use your gifts for others?

 # Doorways of Transition

Sing to the LORD a new song.
(Ps 98:1)

Finally in the sixth grade, Sarah was happy. "Grandma, I was so ready for sixth grade, so finished with grammar school. Middle school is great. You wouldn't believe it. I get to move from class to class, we can leave the school grounds for lunch, and the teachers are great." Breathless, Sarah threw her arms around me, squeezed tight, and almost cried. I had everything I could do not to cry with her. Some transitions are wonderful and exciting. There would be time, I knew, to speak of other less exciting changes. For today she was beaming with joy and I drank it in like the earth welcoming summer rains.

Only a few days after Sarah's joyful proclamation, she stopped by to tell me of her first sixth-grade crisis. Melissa, a classmate not universally liked, was planning to move to another school. While most of her classmates breathed a sigh of relief, Sarah knew how hard it would be for Melissa to move away from school and friends. So Sarah organized a party, sent out invitations, and even decorated. Twenty sixth-graders gathered to mark Melissa's leaving. After an hour of desultory music and chatter, Sarah initiated a ritual, asking each young person there to recount a memory of Melissa. An hour seemed to fly by and when they finished, Sarah told me, "even the boys were crying."

Sarah's joy in entering middle school and instinct about finding a way to celebrate transitions was deeper than even she knew. People need to remember, be grateful, and celebrate passages. Though her classmates were very young, they needed a ritual to help them through their own awkwardness and a forum in which to express themselves. Not only was Melissa touched and helped, all the young people were. Life moves very quickly, especially for our children. There is always one more thing to do, one more event to attend, one more ball game to play. It is too much. Our children and our families need to stop and remember.

The Sunday Eucharist is a weekly reminder to take time to rest, reflect, and gather in gratitude for all God's gifts. In fact, the Eucharist is a transition ritual. We stop to honor and pray for the week gone by, ask for help to live gospel lives in the week ahead, but mostly to rest in the enduring presence of God who is always with us, especially in the gathered assembly. The Sunday Eucharist is a Sabbath that calls us to remember that no matter how cluttered our lives might be, God is always with us, even when we fail to acknowledge God's faithfulness to us and all creation. Sarah's party for Melissa was a Eucharistic moment attuned not only to Melissa's moving but to her classmates' loss of childhood, a kind of grief they did not want even to acknowledge. While most of us stop to listen to those who are hurt, confused, and anxious, Sarah's move to the sixth grade as well as her party and prayer for Melissa, like the Eucharist itself, challenge us to share our joy as well.

Prayer

God of All Transitions,
Ah, the newness of a beginning, singing a new song, breathless,
happy, wonderful, and exciting change! This does not happen

often in my life, God. Or perhaps I simply fail to notice. Let me see again and remember, be grateful and celebrate passages in my own life, and like Sarah, sing joyfully with you. And give me the instincts and courage of a Sarah to celebrate a moving away ritual for another. My heart expands with gratitude for all your gifts, Gracious One. Let me know your presence in the Eucharistic moments of my day. Amen.

Doorway Reflections

- Like this Grandma, how do you drink in the joy of another?
- What loss or grief do you need to acknowledge?
- What is challenging you to share your joy?
- Recall a transition time in your life. In this vulnerable space, who accompanied you as you left the familiar and moved into the unknown? Journal and tell your story.
- What rituals help you to express who and where you are in life and remind you of God's faithful presence?
- In your daily living, what are some of your Eucharistic moments?
- How do you praise God for the goodness within you and the Sarahs of our world?

 # The Stuck Screen Door

Martha was distracted by her many tasks.
(Luke 10:40)

The stuck screen door had been annoying Reisha for weeks, especially when her arms were full of groceries. Determined to fix it, she made a note to herself on a "things to do list" that was already too long. Struck by her own silliness, Reisha knew what she would meditate on the following morning.

Like many of us, Reisha had fallen prey to her own goodness. A mother's helper at her daughter's nursery school, a member of the parish liturgy committee, she had four children under ten, a husband who was working two jobs, and elderly parents to visit at least once a week. Busy was not an adequate description of Reisha's day.

At the same time, Reisha had no idea where or how to cut back. Like the screen door, she was stuck. Though faithful to her daily morning prayer and quiet time, she often found herself looking at the clock as she prayed, anxious to move into the day's activities. Reisha decided to leave the screen door alone for a while, and use it each morning as an image for prayer. Slowly, she began to understand that her door had swollen from too much moisture, just like her life. Unless she found the courage to "shave" the door, and her life, she would be stuck forever.

Jesus addressed people like Reisha more than once. Remember his loving response to Martha's complaint that her sister ought to help her serve her guests: "Martha, Martha, you are worried and distracted about many things" (Luke 10:41). We can hear Jesus say: "Do not let doing define who you are or let it distract you from me. Stop worrying, listen to me, take time for prayer. I am with you always and you do not even notice."

For busy people, Jesus' correction can be difficult to hear. Raised in an environment where hard work is prized, we do our best not to complain about having to do more than our share. At the same time, like the elder brother (Luke 15:29–30), we may sometimes feel that friends and family take us for granted. A wise person once wrote: Don't just do something, sit there. Can we learn to just sit there?

Reisha was determined not to run from her confusion and defensiveness. Breathing deeply, she asked God to help her accept herself as she was, and to learn a deeper sense of gratitude for the all good surrounding her. Her children were healthy, her husband loved her, she was admired in the neighborhood and at church. The only persons she was cheating with her compulsive work habits were God and herself. Reisha, though frightened by her own prayer, asked God for the courage to let go of her "busy as a bee" self-image, and to show her the path to transformation and new growth. There seemed to be no better way to say thank you.

Prayer

God of Being There,
Like the screen door, I am stuck in being busy and in thinking you love me more for what I do than who I am. Give me wisdom to discern what to do, and gratitude for all the good around me. Weaken my compulsive work habits. Help me find time simply to do nothing but be there and here in your love. Amen.

Doorway Reflections

- What does your list of "things to do" look like today? How are you stuck in being busy? Can you learn just to "sit there"?
- Like the annoying screen door, where are you in need of oiling, shaving, letting go, and cutting back?
- Take a moment to discover, attend to and be grateful for the quiet, unhurried moments of your day.

A Praying Place

Jesus was praying in a certain place.
(Luke 11:1)

Cynthia loved the river. She had grown up a stone's throw from its banks, walking along it almost every day. Somehow its constantly changing surface gave her permission to be herself. Some days the river was fierce, choppy, and full of waves, not unlike those troubling moments when she seemed unable to hear others, no matter how loudly they spoke. At other times, it was as smooth as glass, reminding her of those delicious, completely centered moments of contemplation she had holding and rocking her youngest child. Whenever Cynthia felt a real need to get away she would find an excuse to take the short drive to the river, knowing it would eventually give her the space and time to rediscover who she was in the midst of her forever changing life.

All of us need praying places. For some it is a bedroom, for others a garden or walking path. Finding our praying place is one of the first steps toward authentic spiritual health and growth. The Scriptures tell us that Jesus went into the desert and up onto mountains to pray (Matt 14:23; Luke 6:12). Symbolic places in Jewish culture, deserts represented quiet and distance from the distractions of everyday living, and one climbed mountains to be closer to the God who lived in the heavens.

Today, in a church that reinforces the holiness of creation itself (*Catechism of the Catholic Church*, #341), we know that we can be close to God in prayer in any and every place. In the delightful book *Poustinia*, Catherine Doherty reminds us that even crowded and noisy subways can be places of prayer as long as we recognize and attend to the God who always dwells within our own hearts.

In order for this possibility to grow in us, we have first to recognize our need for God on a daily basis. Sometimes when we are doing well in life, when little is out of order or confused, we tend to take our relationship with God and others for granted, expecting them simply to continue and grow without work. When this happens, we find ourselves drifting away from important practices and places. Our prayer is quick, even rushed. In fact, when everything is working well for us, we have a greater need to sit quietly in our praying place, allowing the gratitude for all God's goodness to become deeply planted in our spirits. In this way we will always be able to return to our memory of life's struggles. Praying places are sacred. Finding and treasuring them is one of the first steps on our road to God.

Prayer

God of Sacred Places,
Like the choppy waves or still waters of a river, my life is alter-
nately troubling and calm. Expand my heart space and guide me
to a sacred place where I can rediscover who I am and be with you
in love and gratitude. God of All Praying Places, I welcome you. I
need you. Plant your goodness deep in my spirit. Amen.

Doorway Reflections

- Describe the river of your life today. How and where did you find your praying place? What do you say or do there?
- When are you able to sit and simply be grateful for God's goodness?

 # Doorways for Women

Put out into the deep water.
(Luke 5:4)

"What you are is God's gift to you. What you become is your gift to God." I don't know who first wrote these words, but as a young high school woman I heard them over and over again from Sister Vivian Coulon, a Marianite sister of the Holy Cross. She was one of my first mentors and inspirations and headed our Mission Club at the Academy of the Holy Angels in New Orleans, Louisiana, where I grew up.

Our club met every week, prayed for and discussed the "missions" and peace, had wonderful, fun parties, and challenged us to live our faith a day at a time. Life in Sister Vivian's mind, heart, and Mission Club was challenging to say the least. Kind, compassionate, and understanding, Sister Vivian also demanded a lot from the young women under her care. Because she believed that committed people, especially women, could change the world, she always pushed her students to take one more step, one more chance for the good of the Church and the world. Sister Vivian saw more in us than we saw in ourselves, and every day she encouraged us to lead others to Christ by acts of service and love.

Every time I hear the gospel about Jesus sending Peter into deeper waters, I think of Sister Vivian. Like Jesus, Sister Vivian kept insisting that we find new places to "fish." Not content to "catch" the other students at our high school, Sister Vivian had a much broader vision. She wanted us to put out "into the deep," the uncharted waters of Greater New Orleans and the world. And she was always willing to do the same herself. When she heard of some new need in our school or city, her mind seemed to race for a way to respond. That we, her students and protégés, would follow was taken for granted. Because she believed in us more than we believed in ourselves, we tried anything Sister Vivian suggested!

The world today is a difficult place. Women especially have a long way to go before they reach equality with men in education, health care, a just wage, and so many other human rights. Women work two-thirds of the world's working hours, produce half the world's food, but earn only 10 percent of its income and own only 1 percent of its property. Almost 25 percent of the world's people live in extreme poverty, existing on less than $1 a day. Seventy percent of them are women. From Sister Vivian's perspective one other statistic would be most upsetting. Only 1 percent of the world's women have access to a college education.

Several years ago, at seventy, Sister Vivian took up a new challenge. Leaving New Orleans, not to retire but go to Chiapas, Mexico, she first learned Spanish, then began work among the poor as they struggled for basic necessities. And every year she writes to us, her former students, asking for help. Even as a woman of retirement age she put out into deeper waters because she knew that there were still too many men and women to catch, to influence, to teach. If Jesus came to make the world a more just place, then she had to do her part. Otherwise, we could never hope to build a world with lasting peace.

Prayer

Mentoring God,
You believe in me more than I believe in myself. Help me become
more and more of who I already am—your gift, your life. Allow me
to move from resistance to acceptance of your love. Challenge me

to "*put out into deeper waters*" *and discover new places to "fish."* *Here I am. Send me. Deep gratitude to you, Gifting God, for sending these mentoring people into my life* (name them) *and for the gifts they called forth in me* (name them). *All is yours. Continue to shape and form me and us more deeply in your likeness. Amen.*

Doorway Reflections

- Recall an early mentor in your life and the gifts this mentor called forth from you. What demands were made of you?
- Hear the words of Jesus: "Put out into the deep water" (Luke 5:4). What does this mean for you? Who affirms and sends you into this deeper water, gives you a broader vision of life, and stretches you beyond your comfort zone for the sake of spreading the good news?
- In what peacemaking efforts are you involved? Where do you stand for justice?